A TIME FOR LEARNING

By

Bernice M. Chappel

Copyright 1974
Bernice M. Chappel

ANN ARBOR PUBLISHERS, INC.
P.O. Box 388, Worthington, Ohio 43085

LEARNING PROGRAMS ENGINEERED TO
BEHAVIORAL SPECIFICATIONS

THERE WAS A CHILD WENT FORTH

There was a child went forth
                every day,
And the first object he looked
                upon,
        that object he became,
And that object became part of him
                for the day,
                    or a certain part of the day,
Or for many years, or stretching
                cycles of years.

                        —Walt Whitman

Table Of Contents

Page

Chapter 1: Factors Which Influence Physical And Intellectual Growth 1

The Critical Early Years

    Environmental Influences Shape The Personality And Affect Learning
        Parental Handling Of The Infant, Acceptance By The Siblings And The Emotional Climate Of The Home Have Great Significance

Play And Learning

    Play Is Work For The Infant, Provides An Outlet For Energy And Teaches The Infant About Life
        Infants Learn By Way Of The Senses

The Importance Of Memories

    Feelings That Accompany Facts Constitute Memories
    Memories Are Symbols That Reveal Basic Feelings
    Parents Exert Power In Shaping Memories
    The Importance Of Infant Memories On Behavior In Adulthood
    Significance Of Family Traditions And Rituals
    The Capacity Of The Brain For Storing Information
    The Results Of Memory Experiments Upon The Brains Of Rats

The Importance Of Proper Nutrition

    Stages In The Development Of The Human Brain
        Malnutrition, At Critical Periods, Can Result In Lowered Intellectual Ability
        The Pediatrician Can Be Helpful In Evaluation Of Physical And Intellectual Growth
    Obesity In An Infant May Lead To Obesity In Adult Life
    At Age Three Or Four A Child Is On His Intellectual And Biological Track For Life

Page

Chapter 2: The Family Receives The Baby 5

Parent Relationship

    The Relationship Between Parents Sets The Tone For Family Relationships

        Baby Absorbs Attitudes Of Family Members

Parent-Sibling-Child Relationships

    The Mother-Child Relationship Is The Basis For Adequate Social Adjustment And For The Child To Develop Trust And Affection And The Ability To Relate

    Father-Child And Sibling Relationships Influence The Infant's Personality

Chapter 3: Intelligence 9

Intelligence, What Is It?

    Intelligence Is A Combination Of Inborn Potential Plus Social Development

        Language, The Key To Intelligence

Factors That Influence Intelligence

    The Early Months Of Life Are Crucial If Intelligence Is To Be Increased

    Parents Should Be Warm And Accepting

        Their Attitudes Toward Normal Drives Of The Infant Shape His Personality

        Parental Attitudes Toward Child's Successes And Failures Have A Strong Influence Upon The Child's Attitudes

    A Positive Self-Image Is An Aid To Learning

        Effects Upon Social And Intellectual Success Of Children And Adults

Chapter 4: How Children Learn 14

Learning Requisition

    Learning Involves The Requisition Of New Ways Of Behavior Through Controlled Experiences

Parental Expectations

    Parental Expectations For Child Influence Rate Of Learning

Page

Chapter 4: How Children Learn (continued) 14

Methods Of Learning
Child Learns Through Observation, Listening To Stories, Songs And Rhymes, By Following Directions And Through Non-Verbal Communication Of Family Members

Benefits Of Guided Learning
A More Happy Child
Gratified Parents Who Have Made A Wise Investment In The Child's Future

Dangers To Avoid In Guided Learning
Pressure To Achieve
Competition With Other Children
Activities Beyond The Child's Ability Which May Result In Discouragement And Withdrawal
Activities Too Simple For Child's Ability Do Not Challenge The Intelligence And May Lead To Loss Of Interest

Exceptional Learners
Exceptional Learners Are Those That Deviate Intellectually From What Is Considered Normal Growth And Development

Causes Of Learning Problems
Minimal Brain Dysfunction
Slow Maturation
Emotional Problems
Heredity

Gifted Children
Gifted Children Are Exceptional Learners And Require More Challenging Learning Experiences Than Does The Average Child

Methods Of Teaching
Parents Should Teach Child By Building On His Strengths
- Give Praise When Deserved
- Use Positive Statements
- Avoid Use Of Fear

	Page
Chapter 5: Our Social Behavior	21

Human Values Are The Basic Needs Of People
Values And Attitudes Are Taught Through Parental Example Of Dealing With The Child And Others, Through Play, And By Allowing The Child To Express His Feelings

Values Which May Be Taught
An Empathy For The Feelings Of Others
The Ability To Accept Responsibility
Honesty
Affection
Respect And Courtesy
Tolerance For Minority Groups

Chapter 6: A Guide For Home Training	29

Holding The Child's Interest
Parent Must Hold The Child's Interest If He Is To Learn To The Best Advantage

Suggestions To Stimulate Interest
Use The Democratic Approach
Give Encouragement
Acknowledge Success
Listen To The Child
Hold Frequent Discussions
Help Child To Appreciate The Dignity Of Work
Encourage Creativity
Science And Inquiry Lead To Critical Thinking And Encourage Problem Solving

Avoid Negativeness
Avoid Negative Teaching, Sarcasm, and Severe Criticism Which Are Damaging To The Child's Self-Concept

Activities, Exercises And Games
Explanation Of Suggested Use Of Activities, Exercises And Games For Encouraging The Child To Learn At His Individual Rate

	Page

Chapter 7: Activities, Exercises And Games Which Promote Learning 43

225 Tested Activities, Exercises And Games, Together With Dozens Of Variations And Suggestions Designed To Promote Learning As The Child Is Entertained

Activities Which Interest The Infant 44

    1. The Child's Room
    2. Keep Baby With You
    3. When Baby Is Lonely
    4. Talk To Baby
    5. Music
    6. Naming Objects
    7. Encourage Baby To Touch
    8. Allow Baby Physical Freedom
    9. School Begins At Two Weeks
  10. Motor Activity
  11. Peek-a-Boo
  12. Listening Activities
  13. Crawling Experiences
  14. Word And Object Association
  15. Reading To Baby
  16. Musical Rhythm
  17. Hide And Seek Games
  18. Trips Outside The Home
  19. Continue Talking To Your Child
  20. Playing Games
  21. Continue Reading To Your Child
  22. Records And Radio

Toys 50

  23. Toys

Sensory Experiences For The Three- To Eight-Year-Old ... 52

  24. "Seeing" Without Eyes
  25. Learning And Using Colors
  26. Matching Colors
  27. Jigsaw Puzzle
  28. Foreground And Background
  29. Copy The Design

Page

Sensory Experiences (continued) 52
    30. Learning Shapes
    31. Word Games
    32. Right And Left
    33. Observe As You Drive
    34. Observation And Recall
    35. Look And Learn
    36. Can You Remember?
    37. Instant Recall
    38. Recalling Objects In Order
    39. Similiarities And Differences
    40. Puzzles
    41. Use A Flannelboard
    42. Mazes

Activities Which Develop Coordination 62
    43. Body Size And Shape
    44. The Carpenter
    45. Learning Skills In Dressing
    46. Learning Methods Of Fastening
    47. Writing In The Air
    48. Coordination Training
    49. Motor Skill
    50. A Trace Race
    51. Perceptual-Motor Coordination
    52. Developing Balance
    53. Manuscript Writing

Listening 68
    54. Following Directions
    55. Draw A Picture
    56. Sound Games
    57. High And Low Tones
    58. Are You Listening?
    59. Sounds
    60. Why Listen?
    61. Simon Says
    62. Guided Listening
    63. Over And Under
    64. Which One Is Different?
    65. Do As I Say

Listening (continued) 68
    66. Following Instructions
    67. Can You Catch Me?
    68. Listening For Sounds
    69. How Sharp Are Your Ears?

Communication and Language 73
    70. Language Training
    71. Can You Remember?
    72. Tell The Story Of The Picture
    73. The "Adverb" Game
    74. Communication Skills
    75. Non-Verbal Communication
    76. Verbal Communication
    77. Opposites
    78. Sentence Stories
    79. Completing Stories

Art 77
    80. Craft Materials Stimulate Creativity
    81. Magic Paper
    82. Decorating Trees
    83. An Easy Art Project
    84. Self-Serve Paper

Creativity 80
    85. Enjoyment Of Music
    86. Let's Pretend
    87. Picture Grab Bag
    88. Mind-Stretching Exercises
    89. Make A Story
    90. Tell A Tale

Science 82
    91. Make Science Fun
    92. The Time Concept
    93. What Is It Made Of?
    94. Birds In Winter
    95. Animals In Winter
    96. Shadows

Science (continued) 82

    97. The Wind
    98. Insects
    99. Make A "Bug House"
    100. Where Does It Come From? (1)
    101. Experiments
    102. The Sun's Heat
    103. Outer Space
    104. Where Does It Come From? (2)
    105. Animal, Bird Or Plant
    106. Collections
    107. Magnets
    108. The Seasons
    109. Fact Or Fantasy

Social Behavior 92

    110. Teaching Neatness And Order
    111. Learning About The Family
    112. Television
    113. Role Playing
    114. What Did Mother Do?
    115. Did You Do Something Nice Today?
    116. Being Helpful
    117. What Do Parents Do?
    118. What Work Do They Do?
    119. Who Am I?
    120. Teaching Moral Judgment
    121. Consideration For Others
    122. Think Positively
    123. Fun With The Family
    124. Guess Who
    125. Using The Newspaper
    126. Puppets
    127. Guessing Game
    128. How Would You Feel?
    129. Finish The Story
    130. Likes And Dislikes

Reading And Phonics 100

    131. Stimulate Interest In Reading
    132. Interest In Letter Forms

Page

Reading And Phonics (continued) 100
    133. Teaching The Alphabet, Numerals Or Child's Name
    134. Teaching The Alphabet (continued)
    135. Frame A Letter
    136. Letter Puzzles
    137. Learning About Letters
    138. At The Supermarket
    139. Shopping
    140. Reading Signs
    141. Encouraging Reading And Number Skills
    142. Giants
    143. Tape Recorded Stories
    144. Draw Pictures To Fit The Sounds
    145. How Sharp Are Your Eyes?
    146. Fishing
    147. Letter Bingo
    148. Shortcuts To Reading
    149. Consonant Sounds
    150. Climbing The Hill
    151. Word Recognition
    152. Alphabetical Order Activities
    153. Make A Movie
    154. Missing Letters
    155. Match Them
    156. Sound Grab Bag
    157. Word Hide And Seek
    158. Which Word Doesn't Belong?
    159. I'm Thinking
    160. A Rhyming Guessing Game
    161. I Can Spell!
    162. Word Families And Blends
    163. Practice With Word Endings
    164. Word Family Book
    165. Using The Typewriter
    166. Around And Around We Go
    167. A Sound Wheel
    168. Review Of Consonant Blends
    169. Riddles With Sounds
    170. Finding Little Words In Big Words
    171. Word Games
    172. Scrambled Words

Reading And Phonics (continued) 100
    173. Rhymes And Riddles
    174. Find The Mates
    175. Scrambled Sentences And Stories
    176. Words That Have More Than One Meaning (Homonyms)
    177. The Bookworm
    178. Primary Word Lists

Arithmetic 120
    179. Counting And Identifying Numerals
    180. In The Middle
    181. Comparisons
    182. How Many? (1)
    183. Teaching Numerals (A Quiet Play Activity)
    184. Understanding Numbers
    185. Flannelboard Exercises
    186. Likenesses And Differences
    187. Which Numerals Are Missing?
    188. Follow The Dots
    189. Number Puzzles
    190. Recognizing Numerals And Color Words
    191. Introducing The Addition And Subtraction Concepts
    192. Teaching Addition And Subtraction Concepts
    193. How Many? (2)
    194. Making Comparisons
    195. Learning About Money
    196. Telling Time
    197. Make The Set Match The Numeral
    198. Equivalent Sets
    199. Odd, Even And Equal
    200. Meaningful Numbers
    201. Using The Number Line
    202. Addition And Subtraction Combinations
    203. Put The Scales On The Fish
    204. "Arithmetic" Christmas Tree Ornaments
    205. Counting By 10
    206. Tens And Ones
    207. How Many Steps?
    208. Reading Numerals To 100
    209. Missing Numbers
    210. How Numbers Grow

Page

Arithmetic (continued) 120
    211. Twins
    212. Learning About The Calendar
    213. Ways Of Measuring
    214. Measuring Time

General Knowledge 137
    215. Teaching Cause And Effect
    216. Short Trips Teach The Child
    217. Knowledge Games
    218. Which One Doesn't Belong?
    219. Neighborhood Map
    220. Hurry!
    221. Who Am I? (Riddles)
    222. How People Travel
    223. Traffic Safety
    225. Thinking Of The Future
    225. Categories

Bibliography And Suggested Readings 143

Chapter 1

Factors Which Influence Intellectual And Physical Growth

The first three years are probably the most important period in your child's entire life for during that time while you're helping him develop his intellectual power and desire for learning, his personality is being shaped. In this brief span of time the way in which you handle your child's daily experiences does much to determine his future intellectual and social ability. Consider the thought that the experiences of those early years may determine his success or failure in meeting the challenge of later life. They can turn him into a human who has an excellent chance of doing well in areas which interest him, or they may form him into a social and intellectual failure who can be changed only with difficulty. Though research continues in the field of child development, we now believe that in most cases a child's success or failure in school is determined long before he enters kindergarten.

Human infants have certain basic needs necessary to proper development. Naturally you turn to your pediatrician for direction in the important physical and nutritional areas. Children must be healthy if they are to function at their best intellectual level.

Another basic need of babies is a satisfactory home life which includes acceptance of the child as an individual in an atmosphere where he learns to relate to family members and to gradually acquire the knowledge that he is a worthwhile person. In such an atmosphere a baby will have the opportunity to develop intellectually and emotionally at his own rate.

An infant's random movements and seemingly aimless activities are his earliest methods of learning. You recognize the fact that, to him, play is hard work. Gradually he learns to solve his little problems. Success in solving early childhood problems is his foundation for coping with the complexities of adult life. In play a child learns about the world. He experiments by feeling, smelling, tasting, watching and listening. Play also is an outlet for the excessive energy and troubled feelings of learning to live in a complex world. In play an infant faces many of the everyday tasks of living in the family, and just as his earliest relationships with the family can color his attitudes in later life, so do his early play experiences, particularly his sense of fun.

When we reach back into childhood for memories recalled with the greatest clarity almost always we'll think of experiences or incidents of seemingly minor importance—things which are small in themselves but that carry sharp sensations of joy or warmth, or sometimes of pain. Usually what was important to us was not that we remembered facts, but that we recall the feelings that accompanied the facts. The happiness and sense of security at being held close for the bedtime story, or the comfort of a parent's quiet reassuring voice when we wakened in the dead of night following a frightening dream are feelings we might recall from early childhood. But in spite of the simplicities of our memories, they are the symbols which reveal basic feelings about ourselves, the world, and the reality of life.

The power we parents have to shape our child's memories is a great responsibility. Almost nothing is trivial to a child. Incidents which appear meaningless to us may be the germ of a significant memory on which a child will build.

The human brain can store billions of bits of information, and the bits stored during the early months and years are an important part of the shapers of a child's mind and personality. As an adult he will draw on these early memories as sources of strength—or weakness.

When we are aware that childhood memories can influence our child's adult personality we find inspiration and energy to carry out small plans which are so important to our young child, and we avoid whenever possible, needless disappointment and broken promises. Family rituals, traditions and "special" days often are significant to a child long past the time we might expect. Again, if we think back to our own childhood, we can use our impressions and memories as a guide to ways in which we can influence the memories of our youngster. We can communicate emotions as well as experiences by giving a child memories of warmth and affection, of courage in times of stress, of knowledge and adventure and of pleasure in meeting people and new places. In such memories as these are the roots of feelings and attitudes that will influence a child's approach to life.

Research with rats has been carried on for two decades by psychologists and educators at The University of California at Berkley which has yielded convincing information that the growing animal's psychological environment is of crucial importance for the development of the brain.* The experimenters divided rats into two groups at weaning time. Half were placed in an "intellectually enriched" environment, the other half in a deprived environment. The animals in the first group were given tunnels to explore, levers to press, and ladders to climb while they were cared for and taught with warmth and kindness.
_____

*Today's Education, October 1970. "Don't Use The Kitchen Sink Approach To Enrichment" by David Krech.

As these rats were storing up memories their brother rats in the deprived group lived isolated lives in barren cages with a minimum of intellectual stimulation, though their nutritional needs were met. After 80 days of such treatment the experimenters sacrificed both groups of animals and dissected their brains. The results were convincing. The brains of the rats from the enriched group, who presumably had stored more memories, had a heavier and thicker cortex, a better blood supply and larger brain cells than did the brains of the deprived group. The scientists concluded that by their handling of the young animals they were able to create either "lame brains" or robust active intelligent animals. They concluded also that if there is a parallel between the human and rat brain, stored memories have a direct influence upon the intelligence and dispositions of adults in both areas.

The human brain develops in four stages.* Early intrauterine growth comes from the division of cells at which time the mother's nutrition is of great importance. The brain grows as the cells divide again and again. After birth the cells divide less rapidly but they start growing in size. Near the end of the first year the cells stop dividing altogether. From that time on the cells increase in size but not in number. The final stage in brain development is the forming of connections between the nerve cells. Each cell has about 10,000 connections, and it is likely that the number of connections between the nerve cells is more critical than the number of cells.

Nutrition has a direct effect upon the way both the body and the brain grow. If a fetus doesn't receive enough nourishment the rate of cell division is slowed so that a seriously deprived fetus may have 20% fewer brain cells than a well nourished one. If malnutrition continues during the six months after birth, cell division again is slowed by as much as 20% so that an infant who is malnourished for a few months before and after birth may have only 60% the number of brain cells of a well nourished baby.

Our grandmothers admired fat babies. They thought they were "cute" and said that eventually they'd lose the baby fat. Now we know this idea is false. Dr. Jerome Knittle of New York's Mt. Sinai School of Medicine together with Dr. Jules Hirsh of Rockefeller University have proved in a recent study that fat cells formed in infancy stay in a person's body for life, though the amount of fat a cell is storing may vary from month to month.* They found that the bodies of two-year-olds who had been fat since early infancy contained twice the number of fat cells as did bodies of two-year-olds of

*Life Magazine, December 17, 1971. "Growth: 45 Crucial Months" by Barbara Wyden.

normal weight. The doctors' findings suggest that for the rest of life a person who is fat at age one is going to have a difficult time maintaining normal weight.

Are you wondering where the middle of the road lies in the matter of your child's nutrition? Where you can find the diet which will adequately nourish your baby so that mind and body develop properly, but one which will not result in obesity? We suggest that you consult with the pediatrician at your child's regularly scheduled check-ups. Given a foundation of satisfactory nutrition your child should follow his individual course of physical development which may not parallel that of your friend's baby, or even that of a sibling. The calendar is a poor measurement of a child's progress.

By the time a child reaches three or four years of age he is set on his intellectual and biological track. Unless an accident or serious illness strikes, he will proceed along physical and intellectual growth paths which are now set, and how well he does toward reaching his inborn potential depends to a large extent on the care, training and nutrition of the early months of his life.

Chapter 2

The Family Receives The Baby

How do you begin to teach your child the ABC's of mental health? How can you help him to progress in the ability to relate to others, to develop a healthy self image, to accept responsibility and to listen effectively so that eventually he can solve everyday problems of living? If you approach the guidance of your baby as a pleasant challenge to your ingenuity, as an intriguing undertaking which is your number one priority during his early years, your child should make fine progress.

An important element in influencing a child toward a happy productive life is the atmosphere within the home. The relationship between parents establishes the pattern for relationships within the family. When parents are cooperative and pleasant their children tend to absorb these traits of personality. Whatever the family atmosphere, calm or chaotic, cooperative or antagonistic, it presents its pattern to the children as a standard of life. Strong families produce strong children. A family in which each parent assumes responsibility for his duties, knows and respects his limits and is able to communicate with family members, tends to maintain a feeling of emotional togetherness. Such a home is a haven where children feel secure.

Long before he can think consciously on the verbal level an infant forms attitudes towards what he experiences. He interprets, in a vague way, the happenings of his daily life and draws conclusions which influence his actions. What he is born with intellectually may be less important than what he does with it, for his attitude toward life is the key to his personality. A baby's behavior springs not from rational thought but more from basic partially conscious attitudes toward what is happening to him. At first he operates by trial and error, then whatever he finds to be effective is continued.

Ann Marie, an unsmiling five-month-old infant was two years younger than her bright active brother, Jeffrey. He constantly challenged his mother who was determined that he would "shape up." There was much shouting between mother and child with temper displays by Jeffrey which resulted in frequent spankings. Ann Marie almost never cried but would lie quietly in her crib for hours on end. When Jeffrey screamed and the mother shouted, Ann Marie drew a quivering breath and quietly turned her face to the wall. The pattern continued during her early years with

Jeffrey constantly demanding maternal attention. Meanwhile the baby grew into a passive, fat infant who made little effort to use her mental or physical powers choosing rather to lie or sit quietly, no doubt observing that maternal wrath descended on her brother only when he was verbal, active or noisy. By age four Ann Marie talked very little, and in addition, she had a bad speech defect. She was backward in most areas, and she was obese. Jeffrey, at the head of his first grade class academically, was poorly adjusted socially.

Six years later both children are following the early pattern of behavior. Jeffrey is doing excellent work in school though he continues to challenge authority. Ann Marie, obese and unmotivated, sits out her days in the classroom, hoping to be unnoticed if she does nothing to attract attention. For these children, their intellectual and biological pattern was determined in the early years of life. Children who are denied fondling, happy faces, and loving words during the first three years are more prone to grow up with emotional problems which stunt intellectual growth.

Instinctively most mothers cuddle their infants and talk to and smile at them, which indicates to the baby that he is loved. He enjoys the closeness of the mother and as he senses her happiness in caring for him he quickly learns she can be trusted to be there when he needs her.

Authorities do not agree on the need for a regular schedule in caring for young children, but many, including Dr. Peter Neubauer, director of the Child Development Center in New York, stress the importance of establishing a baby's trust in the early days of life.* He emphasizes a child's need for "continuity of care, rather than the care itself, so that he can anticipate next the events and learn what are the sequences of his condition." Thus the baby's confidence grows as he learns his mother will feed him when he is hungry and that she will bathe him and change his diaper and generally make him comfortable. This is the manner in which the mother-child relationship is formed. There is unanimous agreement among authorities in the mental health field that an early mother-child relationship is of primary importance in shaping the emotional life of a child. At six to eight weeks most babies reward their parents with a smile which is a significant landmark in the child's development, for he then recognizes familiar faces and associates them with feelings of pleasure. We know that seriously neglected children do not smile, and believe that smiling is not an inborn trait but comes as a response to a pleasant experience.

*Life Magazine, December 17, 1971. "Yes to Love And Joyful Faces" by Vivian Cadden.

Though a father's time with the baby is limited, the relationship with his child has a powerful influence upon the youngster's emotional development. In contrast to former years, today there is an increasing tendency to include the father in planning for the birth of his baby. He attends lectures about infant care so that when the baby arrives he emotionally joins with the mother in welcoming the infant. A father's early association with his baby helps to lay the groundwork for trust and confidence. Often a father's contact with a child tends to balance the mother's inclination to be over-protective. Boys, in particular, need a strong male figure to look up to and respect—a pattern for manhood.

New born infants are influenced by adult handling from the first hour of birth. As soon as it is permitted the father as well as the mother should hold and cuddle the little one so that he senses their friendly acceptance. To be kindly treated and welcomed is bound to set up positive feelings of trust and confidence that makes the world seem like a friendly place.

Don't be concerned that you will "spoil" your child. Relaxed friendliness and acceptance of his needs will not spoil a baby. By experiencing love and cooperation from his parents he develops a first hand feeling for these traits and becomes trusting and friendly in return. In contrast, children who are deprived of love and who are frustrated by rejection in infancy are less able to be loving and giving as they grow older.

If parental acceptance is of primary importance, so is the manner in which the new baby is received by the elder children. Without adequate preparation for the new arrival the older child is likely to give the infant who usurps his place somewhat less than a warm welcome. Problems can be avoided if months before the birth of the baby the elder children are included in planning for the new arrival. It usually is effective if you stress your need for their help in caring for the baby, and if you often point out the fact that when they were infants you planned for their birth and cared for them just as you will for the new baby—only then you did it without the help of "big brothers or sisters."

Nancy is the third of five children. A third baby in a three year period was looked upon as an unfortunate "accident" by Mrs. B., but when the child was a third girl the mother was completely rejecting, at first refusing even to look at the baby. At home the two toddlers likewise viewed the newcomer as an intruder and she was subjected to constant reminders that she was unwanted.

Mr. B., a business man who worked long hours, seemed helpless to change the situation in the short amount of time he was at home.

Meanwhile Nancy developed into a cross baby, which fact did nothing to endear her to her mother and sisters. At an early age she was verbally and physically abused in an attempt to change her "disagreeable disposition." A year later the family's long-hoped-for boy was born, and three years later the last of the siblings, another girl, arrived.

Nancy remained the scapegoat, and as a result she did not learn to properly relate to children. She was in constant trouble at home, in the neighborhood and in school.

Teachers and a school social worker are attempting to help her work through her problems, but progress is poor and chances for their resolution are not good. Mrs. B. and the siblings are still vehement in their expression of her "meanness, deceit and sloppy appearance." They're unable to recognize the fact that Nancy is what they have made her. Mr. B. is verbally cooperative but is ineffective in bringing about change within the home.

And what does the future hold for Nancy? School people fear she will never be able to use her adequate intelligence effectively since she is using most of her time and energy attempting to "get even with the world," which results in increasingly serious involvement. She is a bitter, unloved eleven-year-old child on a vicious treadmill.

We can only conclude that from the moment of birth the family atmosphere and pattern of living have a strong influence upon a child's behavior, intelligence and personality.

Chapter 3
Intelligence

The aim in early training of children is to stimulate their curiosity so that they will strive to learn more about matters which hold their interest. Daily contact with a cheerful parent who makes demands just enough above the child's level of ability to be interesting and who appreciates his every success is an incentive to the child to work hard and to really learn. Just as an infant's muscular development depends upon exercise, so does his rate of intellectual development depend upon stimulating mind-stretching exercise.

What precisely is intelligence? Intelligence, like language is largely a social factor. It is a combination of human inborn potentialities coupled with social development, and both elements wait for needs or interests to prod them into action. What any human has done, all can do to a degree, and the extent of the degree depends upon how great an interest the person has in training his potential. Intelligence is only a means of getting to a desired end.

In discussing intelligence we should mention psychological testing and the I.Q. If you're confused about the I.Q., you're in good company for even some psychologists who have been administering intelligence tests for years entertain serious doubts about the usefulness of such tests in predicting a child's performance. In our discussion we're not concerned with a magic numerical score which is supposed to measure your child's intelligence. Unless you and the pediatrician see signs of unusually slow mental development psychological evaluation generally is unnecessary in pre-school children.

A child's capacity to learn is not fixed at birth, but if we are to boost the intelligence we must begin when the child is very young. Authorities differ as to the time span of the golden months for increasing the intelligence, some believing that the time between the 10th and the 18th months is the most decisive. Nearly all agree that the trend or pattern of learning is set by age four, and many authorities incline toward a younger age.*

The most important key to your child's intelligence is language. Human thought is based upon language and on the manipulation of symbols (letters, numerals, etc.) which represent ideas, things and

*Life Magazine, December 17, 1971. "A Child's Mind Is Shaped By Age Two" by Maya Pines.

*Parents Magazine, September, 1970. "The Crucial Years For Learning" by Cynthia Lang. (Based upon Dr. Burton L. White's Pre-School Project at Harvard University.)

relationships. Children who live in homes where communication is inadequate start kindergarten with a handicap. Their intelligence is inclined to be low so that they soon fall behind and they often fail to catch up with their more fortunate classmates. As adults they still are behind for our modern world appears to have little use for people with meager skills.

When is the right time to stimulate the curiosity and interest of a child? The first few days of life are not too soon, and language is the key. Talk to your baby. Talk to him when you feed him, when you bathe, dress and change him. Talk to him as you go about your housework. Surround him with natural talk used freely. At this stage of development he doesn't understand the words but you are showing him that people communicate by facial expression and tone of voice as well as by the use of language. In addition, he senses your interest and attention. You are providing stimulation which can produce changes in the functioning of your child's brain.

Parents within a warm understanding home are a child's first, best and most successful teachers. They teach by example, by creating an environment which arouses the child's interest, by listening with attention and explaining when helpful, by loving him, by introducing him to the fascination of the world and by taking advantage of each opportunity for learning as it presents itself. You'll notice that most of the methods of teaching a child are accomplished with the help of language, the key which unlocks intelligence. It is the means by which humans acquire, preserve and transmit thought. Every area of our existence depends upon language for the transmission of ideas and information. In this modern age and in a nation where the responsibilities of the country lie with the voting citizen we need to prepare our children for the ability to read with discrimination, write with clarity and to communicate effectively with fellow citizens; in these areas language is the key to success.

During the early months when rapid learning takes place and a child's environment largely determines how much of his genetic potential will be realized, parents should be alert to possibilities for stimulating the baby's thinking. The cortex of the human brain can be roughly compared to a computer which must be programmed before it can operate effectively. A child's brain is "programmed" by means of sensory stimuli which are sent to it along the nerve pathways from the eyes, ears, nose, mouth and tactile and kinesthetic senses. The more sensory stimuli with which the brain is activated the greater will be its ability to function.

Because there is a time limit when brain cells divide and are easily activated, parents must not wait but should be alert to their baby's built-in drive to explore, investigate, and to seek excitement by encouraging the infant to use all of the senses as a means of satisfying his boundless curiosity. Parents sometimes fail to recognize curiosity as an indication of intelligence and the behavior of toddlers is misinterpreted as "naughtiness." Rather than a slapped hand, which stifles the child's interest, he should be helped to find outlets which encourage appropriate investigation.

If you experiment you'll find that when your baby is a few days old he will react to a simple brightly colored object such as a red balloon, when it is held before his face. His eyes will focus as they rest upon the object and his body becomes alert. The reaction will occur when he again is shown the same brightly colored object, but eventually the novelty will wear off and he will give more attention to a different object.

In the early days following birth some infants pay attention to a drawing of a face. The behavior of rapidly losing interest may indicate the child's mind can concentrate on one thing for only a brief span of time because his brain urgently needs more stimulation due to the drive to pay attention to many things. As parents we need to help youngsters satisfy the need to look, to experiment, to explore and to experience a variety of stimuli, for then the baby not only will learn but he will be more happy. When your child is fed, dry, comfortable and healthy, if he's fussing, perhaps he has the need for new sensory stimuli. The busy interested youngster who is learning new things usually is a happy child.

Children have an inborn desire to learn how to do things. They handle, manipulate, investigate and try to master their environment primarily because they find such activity enjoyable. For them learning is fun, and they will continue their efforts unless they are discouraged by pressure, competition, punishment or fear.

If you keep in mind that learning is fun for your small child you have a guide for planning mentally stimulating activities that aren't too immature or advanced, too easy or difficult. The purpose of the activities which will come to your mind, as well as the planned intellectual growth exercises found in Chapter Seven, is not to push or pressure the youngster to compete with a neighbor's or relative's child, but only to cause him to be interested and happy as he learns about the world.

Eric's parents had provided mind-stretching exercises from the day of his birth and as they pointed out interesting things they talked to him about them. At age two Eric was taken on a ferry boat to an amusement park where he enjoyed rides and treats. Later when his grandmother inquired what he'd liked about the trip he immediately replied, "Engine!" Eric's father explained the child had been engrossed in watching the operation of the boat engine and that of all the things he'd done that day, the engine had most interested him.

If you are to meet the intellectual needs of your child, the emotional atmosphere of the home must be such that the baby is motivated to learn. The attitude toward the youngster should be warm and democratic rather than cold and authoritarian. In homes where parents are warm and loving, where they take time to explain and let children make decisions of which they are capable, and where the children are encouraged to develop their intellect through experimentation and discovery, each child is more likely to progress because the ingredients are present which feed and nourish his developing intelligence.

It's not necessary that you be completely permissive nor that you allow your child to run wild. Neither should he interfere with the rights and possessions of others. Your home need not be child-centered, but we do advocate that you let your child know you love him wholeheartedly even though firmly and kindly you insist that he respect the rights of others in the family. And he needs as much voice in decisions involving him as he can handle. Keep in mind that your goal is to develop a thinking individual. A two-year-old is capable of deciding whether he prefers corn flakes or oatmeal for breakfast and whether he wants to wear the red or blue sweater.

All homes need guidelines and rules for smooth functioning. It helps if you explain to your toddler the "whys" behind the few necessary rules you have set up and the decisions which you enforce. Your child will learn to evaluate alternatives and over a period of time he'll gradually accumulate information upon which to make decisions.

If humans are to use their intellects most advantageously, they must have a good self-concept, for liking one's self is the foundation for intellectual and emotional growth. A child needs adult help to develop and maintain a positive self-image which will enable him to continue liking himself from childhood and through to adulthood. The way a child feels about himself usually is the key to his entire life for it influences the kinds of friends he chooses, how he gets along with others, and how productive he will be. Self-respect is based upon whether or not a person feels he is lovable and worth while, and these needs are vastly more important to a small child than to an adult. A positive self-image is a child's most valuable possession.

Children learn by trying new things, but certainly each effort will not meet with success. As parents we can do a lot to help our child by encouraging him to think through problems and to make decisions of which he is capable. In the frenetic tempo of modern life we should stimulate our child to be more self-reliant, for self-reliance will help him to successfully meet the demands of society. He needs guidance and encouragement to struggle with a problem which at his level of maturity he is capable of solving. When he is successful his joy is doubly rewarding if you join in recognition of his worthwhile achievement.

And when he fails, a parent can encourage without criticism while giving hints which will lead the child to try again, or sometimes to try a new approach. There is a vast difference between guiding a child in a difficult project or doing everything for him. In the former approach the youngster will feel the joy of achievement in success; in the latter he may decide the activity was too difficult for him and that he wasn't "smart enough" to be successful. Repeated failures may lead to a low self-image, while frequent successes cause a child to feel gratification in his achievement and confidence in his ability resulting in a glow of happiness.

Regardless of the intellectual level, a youngster's general disposition, personality and emotional well-being are largely the products of his feelings about himself and his family's acceptance and reactions to him in everyday life. The experiences each day gradually build the character of tomorrow. You'll note that the more new things your child has seen and heard, the more new things he wants to experience. And the greater the variety of activities with which he has coped, the greater is his capacity for coping. Stimulating changes in the environment develop the brain.

To help a child realize his greatest intellectual and social potential, then, we should stimulate his thinking through early sensory experiences, through talking, demonstrations, and parental example, and by warm acceptance of him as a person so that he is motivated to learn as he solves new and challenging problems.

Chapter 4
How Children Learn

What is learning? In the broadest sense learning involves the acquiring of new ways of behaving—that is, new patterns of feeling, acting and thinking that are gained through more or less controlled experiences.

Some children learn more easily than others. We are uncertain whether the slow learner's behavior is inherent, or the result of lack of interest and unproductive direction of energy, or a lack of effective teaching. Perhaps it is a combination of many factors. As your child's first and most effective teacher you hope to help him learn and to find pleasure in acquiring new skills and knowledge as he absorbs acceptable social attitudes and values. Your expectations for him influence his learning to a great extent. If you expect him to make gains there's a good chance he will progress. It isn't necessarily because he is more capable than another child, but simply that he senses your positive feelings about his ability, and your expectations are transmitted by facial expressions, posture and touch as well as by the spoken word. His response to your positive feelings results in progress, which in turn reinforces your impressions about his "brightness" so that you're motivated to continue feeding him opportunities for learning. The intelligence level of almost every youngster can be raised to a substantial degree by providing a stimulating, loving home environment. And, as might be expected, a parent who has negative feelings and low expectations for a child is likely to realize her expectations since she unconsciously influences her child's behavior in that direction.

When does learning begin to take place? Learning occurs at the time a child sees some behavior that attracts and interests him, or when he wishes to imitate something that catches his fancy. If he wants very much to be successful, and the task is one of which he is mentally and physically capable, he likely will meet with success. It's rare to find a child who can't learn something he wants to learn.

Learning occurs in various ways, one of the most important being from observation of the behavior of parents and siblings. To the young child the family represents the way experienced people meet life. One of the happiest and most successful ways to stimulate a child's mental development is to let him share your interests and activities for as he absorbs knowledge he may also acquire many of your attitudes and values. The common ground for families which produce outstanding sons and daughters is a driving need to be doing, going, and learning as they're involved in challenging ideas and activities. The responsibility for creating a love of learning falls first on the home and is later continued by the school. If the home fails to stimulate this desire we may have a problem learner when a child enters school.

But how can parents influence behavior to insure their child's success as a learner? Much learning is acquired through play. Children learn about the world around them by experimenting and exploring their environment. Infants learn through their senses. They feel, see, hear, smell and taste. Parents can provide new opportunities for learning via the senses by allowing children to experiment, and through trial and error. Unless they are guided, children may experience a degree of "esthetic failure" which is not related to lack of intelligence, but to lack of observation. In such cases the adults may have been uninterested, too busy, or simply unaware that a child may not observe the beauty of a sunset, the fragrance of a flower, the softness of velvet or the whisper of the wind through the pines. Observation, then, is a major method by which children learn, and parents in pointing out interesting environmental facts are training their child in awareness which will enable him to perform better in other intellectual areas.

Usually we think of vision as acuity or sharpness of sight. Actually it is a much broader thing, for though a child may be neither farsighted nor nearsighted, he may not have good vision for he must be able to interpret what he sees, and then act accordingly. In other words, his eyes must act together and relate to the way he coordinates the two sides of his body. There are numerous things which you can do in the first weeks of life to teach your baby to use his eyes properly and to develop coordination. Chapter Seven contains suggestions for such activities.

In childhood and in adult life listening skills are a vital necessity in this verbal world. Half of a child's time in school is spent in listening. He listens to stories, directions, announcements, recordings, radio and television programs, lectures and sound films. But he needs to do more than hear the material presented or else his time is wasted. He must comprehend and understand what is said. You can teach your child to listen with understanding. Two factors are necessary for effective listening, interest and a purpose for listening.

A time-tested method which teaches proper listening habits is found in the use of stories, jingles, rhymes and songs. From the earliest weeks of life your child will enjoy simple songs and nursery rhymes. He won't understand the words but he will derive joy from the personal attention and the sound of your voice. Nursery rhymes and songs teach rhythm and soon become part of a child's memory.

A few months later your child will enjoy sitting in your lap and turning the pages of brightly colored cloth or cardboard books as you point out details in the pictures and read the simple stories. Don't expect a young child to sit for more than a few minutes. When his interest wanes, terminate the story period. Never insist that he "sit still and listen." Listening to stories shouldn't be just a bedtime activity, either. Try various times of day, or take a book and read under a shady tree, or in the park.

Most fathers spend very little time with their children during the work week. Perhaps the bedtime story period should be reserved for father as it may be the one time during the day when a youngster can claim his father's undivided attention. A short "mini-tale" can do a great deal for a child as it educates and entertains, and it is a pleasant relaxing way for a busy father to get to know his child.

A reverence for books can be taught during the toddler stage when a child graduates from the cloth and cardboard type to the usual paper books. Show him how to turn pages carefully as you read to him, and by age three, or perhaps earlier, he'll enjoy trips with you to the public library to select his own stories. Just seeing books around the house makes children wonder what's in them. Through books, then, we can stimulate a child's listening ability in early life while he gains knowledge and acquires the idea that reading and learning are fun.

Let's remember that listening should be a two-way street. Too often we parents fail to listen to our children. We are likely to *talk at* children rather than to listen to them. If we'd encourage them to ask questions and to express ideas and feelings, we'd stimulate their thinking more than when we "preach."

The depth and extent of information of three-, four- and five-year-olds is greater than we generally realize. Children not only crave great amounts of information and knowledge, but they enjoy using it. For young children the greatest resource is adults who listen to them and who talk to them about ideas, and who provide opportunities for them to develop further understanding through play experience.

While children learn from observation and listening they also gain a great amount of knowledge from doing, which includes experimenting. Much of such learning is done by the trial and error method, but ideas and skills learned by doing are likely to be retained. Whenever possible allow your youngster to learn by this approach for he'll be thrilled when he discovers new facts. A simple example of learning by doing is blowing soap bubbles. Your youngster may enjoy watching you produce beautiful bubbles, but even though you explain how he should proceed, until he tries several times, learning by doing is the only method which can bring him success. Eventually success will lead to "why" questions, which is your opportunity to give simple facts about air pressure in soap bubbles, balloons and tires. Toddlers are the most intellectually alert of all humans. Unfortunately adults too often stifle these talents instead of developing them.

Non-verbal communication, or transmitting ideas by facial expressions, body posture or gesture is recognized as a method of learning. Consider your silent reaction to pleasant experiences. Your facial expression and posture tell everyone within sight that you're enjoying what you're doing. Now consider your reaction to an unpleasant sight, sound, smell or taste. Do you doubt that your observant child would understand the message you transmit?

Because young children can't sit still for long, most pre-school learning takes place on the go. If a person's achievement in life depends largely upon information he has learned before age three or four, then it is clear that the home and not the school is the country's major educational institution. We need to make the home an effective learning center for it is here that our children's earliest thoughts and memories are conceived—thoughts and memories which will have profound consequences and effects upon their later years.

The toddler's zest for life and learning and the breathless excitement of trying and succeeding at new things is an asset which parents should utilize to the maximum if the child is to realize his intellectual potential, as well as to grow in self-confidence. It appears that the more new things a child has seen and heard, the more he wants to see and hear. The crucial problem is to find the most stimulating circumstance at each point of development. Given anything too difficult and a child will withdraw or ignore it; anything too familiar, and he has no interest. The trick is to find something just a trifle beyond knowledge he already has stored in his brain so that he must stretch a bit to achieve success. During the all-important first months and years, then, we should try to manage the child's life in such a way that he is interested and enjoys life. Appropriate guided stimulation never harms a child. There is, however, danger in using new theories about intellectual development to cause a youngster to compete with a relative's or neighbor's child, or where approval or affection is withheld unless the child performs. Such an approach to learning leaves the youngster feeling worthless and driven to achievement by fear of failure instead of being motivated through interest from within himself. But if you, the child's most important lifetime teacher, guide him in learning at his own pace, he will progress, for in the home he won't face the competition, academic pressure, formal timetable for learning and fear of humiliating public mistakes which handicap many children in the schoolroom. And, at home you can provide the immediate feedback of praise and correction which is necessary in the learning process.

Because children grow at different rates mentally as well as physically, your child may not follow the usual pattern of development. Many thousands of American parents are seriously concerned about the poor academic achievement of their children. There is justification for their concern for one in seven elementary schoolchildren (and one in four in large city elementary schools) requires special attention to keep up with his classmates in reading.*

Learning deficiencies are not confined to reading or to children living in poverty. Failures occur in all skill subjects and in children from all types of homes. Causes for learning deficiencies may be mental retardation, emotional disturbances, educational deprivation, lack of motivation or poor teaching. But in addition to the children whose learning problems are due to the above causes, most classrooms contain from one to three children whose academic progress is not in keeping with their mental ability which may be in the superior range. These children have problems called specific learning disabilities. About one in every fifteen children in United States schools is handicapped in this way.*

What are specific learning disabilities? The child with such a problem is handicapped by neurological impairment which results in minimal brain dysfunction, and as a result he may have trouble with physical coordination or in seeing, hearing, comprehending, remembering and controlling his behavior.

The seeing or hearing impairments differ from the usual problems in that though vision is 20/20 and the hearing loss is zero on the audiometer, the child is unable to perceive minute differences in the shapes of letters and numerals and he is unable to perceive differences in similar phonetic sounds. Since reading involves the use of letters and sounds, minor problems in perceiving them makes reading an extremely difficult process for children with specific learning disabilities.

There are numerous theories as to the causes of specific learning disabilities. Some psychologists claim such difficulties are emotional in nature, while neurologists are inclined to cite brain damage as the chief cause. Heredity is another factor which is mentioned. Many experts think this type of learning problem is caused by mental immaturity, a delay or unevenness in the full development of those

*Today's Education, January 1972, "Specific Learning Disabilities"

functions of the brain that help us to interpret the sights and sounds which make up speech and reading, and which enable us to carry out tasks which require muscular coordination.

It is interesting to note that the larger number of children who have specific learning disabilities are boys. We believe heredity is sometimes related to the problem since frequently a father and son both are handicapped with a severe reading problem. Other causes of specific learning disabilities may be long and difficult labor preceding birth, illness in the early months of life with prolonged high temperature, or a serious head injury.

It is likely that your child does not have a specific learning disability, but regardless of whether or not he does he'll profit from activities which are designed to encourage development of the visual, auditory and tactile senses, as well as exercises which encourage training in muscular coordination such as are presented in Chapter Seven.

You may be the parent of an unusually bright or gifted child. Such a youngster is a challenge for he requires more stories, activities, experiments and explanations to occupy his active mind than does the average child. You note as you expose him to new experiences that his perception is excellent and he rapidly learns his letters and numbers. He recognizes signs and different cars when he sees them on the street. He is thirsty for new knowledge and activities.

Are you thinking, "But I have other children and a home to care for. I don't have the time to be a teacher, too." It takes no longer to think in terms of guiding a youngster's learning than it does to operate chiefly as his caretaker, and it certainly is more pleasant for both of you. Because a young child's attention span is short it's not necessary to hunt for big blocks of time in your day in order to help him learn. As a tiny infant you can entertain him while changing diapers by singing a song, repeating nursery rhymes or calling attention to a toy, picture or pet. When he's older you can play word games as you work about the house. While driving you can count red cars, green cars, orange trucks or stop lights. You can keep a mental file of ideas for times when he is likely to fuss, such times as waiting for the doctor or saleslady. Whatever amount of time you are able to invest will pay dividends for your child later on, and it will make for a more pleasant relationship between you now.

Another way to aid your child's mental development is to make praise, encouragement and love your chief methods of discipline. These techniques work effectively in helping intellectual, social and emotional growth. No matter how annoying a child, you can find opportune moments to praise him for something he is doing right; in this way you'll teach him to work from strength, not weakness and discouragement.

Some parents set standards so high that their children never can satisfy them. Then youngsters feel inadequate and stop trying and the parent becomes even more critical. Children have great respect for their parents' judgment. If they're told they're "stupid" or the "naughtiest child on the block," they are almost certain to believe the statements and quite likely will behave accordingly. Because your child believes what you say about him, statements such as the following help to foster a self-image that will enable him to learn without dragging self-doubt. You might say, "This is hard, but you've always enjoyed doing hard things. I remember how you worked when you were a baby to learn to sit up and then to creep and walk. You never stopped trying." Or, "I enjoyed having lunch with you at the restaurant. The waitress was slow but you waited nicely." Or, "You're really growing up. I was proud of the way you pushed the cart and helped me find the groceries at the supermarket." Positive statements work wonders in influencing your child's social behavior and joy in learning.

In encouraging a child to learn we should keep in mind two important facts: first, that vital, vivid, pleasant experiences are the easiest to remember, and second, memory works best when it's unforced. Just as we think poorly when we're anxious or afraid, so do children stop learning when they're fearful. Fear of failure, of disappointing you, of scolding, of spanking, of withdrawal of your love or of unmentioned future consequences are poor ways to induce desirable behavior. Rather, encourage your child to try, and let him know that you don't consider failure a crime, but that it is one way of learning what *doesn't* work.

As you satisfy your child's urgent need to learn and understand you'll find he is more happy and easier to manage and so will present fewer discipline problems, because as he experiments and learns he has an outlet for his restless curiosity. You'll enjoy your child more too, for parents can't help enjoying their child's pleasure in learning. A wonderful emotional relationship grows up between you when you act as guide and the two of you explore a fascinating world. Later, as an adolescent and young adult, your child likely will feel less need to rebel against you or to make a clean break for independence which is so common in young people.

So regardless of whether your youngster seems to be a slow, average or fast learner, enjoy him. Have fun together as he grows in experience with the freedom you give him to broaden his potentials. All children, whatever the level of intelligence, will grow mentally if they're warmly taught.

Chapter 5
Our Social Behavior

Society is suffering from a kind of value vertigo. We are in a state of confusion about values and respect for money, law and order, property, religion and race. It seems that we are lacking in empathy for others. We need to "get inside the other person's skin" to try to realize how he feels. Only then can we have sympathy for the unfortunate and an understanding of why people act as they do in various situations.

If we select one word that characterizes life in the latter part of the twentieth century, that word likely would be "change." To live fulfilling lives our children must be able to adapt to change. As the population increases they must learn to live harmoniously in closer quarters. New skills will be required as technological advances abolish some occupations and create others. Tomorrow's adults will need to know how to make constructive use of free time. And the twenty-first century promises even more far-reaching changes which will affect all members of society.

Adapting to change requires flexibility. This quality is possible if a person has a realistic sense of his own dignity and worth and if he consciously makes an effort to assume responsibility for his welfare and for the welfare of others.

Our ideas of child-raising are based upon things we believe in—values that consciously or unconsciously we transmit to our children. Our aim is to mold the children's behavior so that they can live comfortably within the family and later so that they can live in the world outside the family with some semblance of order. Children constantly observe their parents. They see how we talk to each other and how we cooperate and show consideration for family members. Gradually they're aware that when people behave decently, life is much more pleasant.

What specifically are human values? We consider values to be the universal basic needs and wants of human beings. Each person, beginning early in childhood, needs to attain a realistic sense of his own worth and to recognize and respect the feelings and rights of others. A person's sense of his own worth, the self-image which is developed early in life, is dependent upon the degree to which he is able to satisfy his basic wants and needs. Seriously frustrated humans who are unable to view themselves as worth-while persons cannot attain their full potential either socially or intellectually.

Children need to be taught the social behavior which will help them to live more harmoniously in our society in such a way that their basic needs are satisfied without depriving others of their rights. Such teaching will help them to better understand human behavior—their own and that of others.

How do we go about teaching basic values and attitudes? Your child will live with you exactly as you live with him. When you set reasonable limits and objectives for the family, you set the pace, and your child will not be far behind. The attitudes and behavior that are learned in his early years become the foundation upon which the rest of his life is built. The most important method of teaching values, then, is by your example in dealing with your child and with others. The way you live with the child—what you expect of him—teaches him the facts of life. He doesn't learn from "telling" for telling isn't training. He needs to learn that living means to help. Parents who give all and ask nothing soon produce a child who expects everything and gives nothing.

In every family there is a hidden dimension which is the feelings of the family members. Many parents tend to ignore the feelings of their child. To do so is to ignore a large part of the real world for there are few things that humans do that are not, in one way or another, shaped by emotions. The person who understands his feelings and who is not afraid to express them is a better human, for feelings are at the heart of a person's identity, both as he is viewed by himself and others. Encourage your child to express his feelings. Tell him you may not agree with him but that he has a right to say how he feels. Try to help him to think positively and to express positive feelings as well as negative ones. After he has had an opportunity to vent frustration and anger, ask him to think what he likes about this particular person. If he wishes to continue in a negative manner, suggest that he has made his point, then repeat that you'd like him to think of something he likes about the person being discussed. If he's unable to do so, you might express your opinion about an admirable quality of the person. Try to end the conversation on a positive note.

Your child should be given the freedom to follow his interests and to freely express his feelings so long as family and home are not sacrificed. He needs to learn that for every right there is a responsibility, for rights and responsibilities are tied together.

Present day young people are finding the kind of freedom they have never experienced before. For the majority, life has given them very little practice in taking responsibility for their actions. To many of them freedom means doing what they want, when they want, without having to account to anyone. The lucky bright ones learn they can't have it both ways—all freedom and no responsibility.

All children are in search of limits. Subconsciously they like the security of knowing parents will not permit them to physically or emotionally hurt themselves or others. When you allow your child to have his little problems and to experience limitations appropriate to his age, you are training him for maturity, for he comes to understand that in the give and take of life he has to do his share of giving and must learn to accept his share of difficulties.

Child raising, like any worthwhile task, must have a plan. While you encourage your child to make suggestions, it is for you to make final decisions in important matters. Many times insecurity in a child results from his lack of knowledge of the limits of his authority and responsibility. The child who invariably gets his way will be insecure for he has found no limits anywhere. "Protective limits" then, should be started at an early age for they cause a child to be secure in the knowledge that a loved and wiser parent will have the final decision in matters of significant importance.

Gradually as children grow in maturity and ability to make decisions, parents need to free themselves from their child's dependency. Perhaps it will be easier if you remember that every type of immature behavior displayed by a capable child has at its core the desire to secure personal advantage without giving anything in return. A child who is allowed undeserved privileges is being trained for failure in life. The youngster for whom repeated parental sacrifices are made usually becomes more and more selfish as a result, and the selfish child is headed for trouble and unhappiness.

Gradually a youngster should learn to rely more upon himself. Society demands only two things, that we maintain ourselves and that we do not burden others. A child who leans on others can go no farther than others are willing to carry him. Everyone, parents included, eventually becomes fed up with the demanding child. Children need to learn that life's tasks depend on teamwork which involves each one doing his task completely. No relationship, even the parent-child one, can be advantageous if it is lacking in mutual advantage. Most youngsters have a keen sense of fair play and are less likely to object to disagreeable things if they are fair. They need to know the proper limits in relationships within the family, for uncertainty leads to discontent.

We parents, then, should not do anything for a child that he is physically and mentally able to do for himself. Generally, children would grow up with little difficulty if parents interfered less with them. If we could but give a little less help each day, the child might struggle a bit at times but this struggle prepares him for the frustrations he'll find outside the home. Gradually he will accept the responsibility for helping himself, and in the success from conquering new tasks he discovers the pleasures of independence.

Are you wondering what your child's ability to accept responsibility for his actions has to do with teaching him to use his intellectual potential? There is a relationship. Children who enter school unable to care for their physical needs or to interact appropriately with classmates may lose confidence in their ability. They see themselves as inadequate individuals—they don't like themselves. This low self-image influences their success in primary grade learning activities so that they may fall behind. Failure in school may not indicate lack of intelligence as much as lack of confidence under stress. So the earlier your child can accept responsibility for himself, the earlier his interests and intelligence will be freed for other learning.

A self-reliant child takes pride in demonstrating how much he can do unaided. He finds no satisfaction in disrupting others to force them to be attentive. He discovers ways to occupy himself rather than to occupy others. He looks forward to growing up and enjoys tackling things a bit too advanced for him. How does he gain the character and qualities of a self-reliant child? He learns from us by the way we live with him.

Truth appears to be a lost virtue in our commercialized life. Adults can sift the truth from lies, a child cannot. He believes what he sees and what he is told. Just as a baby learns courage from dealing with minor frustrations, he learns the truth by experimenting, and when he can speak by asking, "What is this? What is that? Why? Why? Why?" He is trying to find out the truth. And though at times you are tired of his questions, give him a truthful answer. Half-truths and lies cause him to lose faith in you, for you're saying by example that lying is acceptable behavior.

And as you're completely truthful in answering your child's questions in simple short answers, so must you be just as cautious about making and keeping promises or meeting difficult situations which the child may dislike. Such experiences as bedtime, going to the doctor and dentist or to the hospital are easier for the child who is prepared for them by his parents. Even the most difficult truth of all—the truth of death—must be told.

Truth is important to a child because it sets him free from false anxiety and helps him to cope with the situation. For example, the regular medical checkup with the possibility of shots is dreaded by most children. Unless they're certain, parents shouldn't promise the child there will not be shots. Instead, they might say something like, "I guess none of us likes shots for they hurt for a minute, but sometimes we need them to help us to stay healthy." Such an explanation prepares a child for an unpleasant experience, and he is taught that he can rely on what parents say.

Though you are truthful with your child and promises are kept in the home, when he leaves your side he'll hear lies and half-truths from other children and adults. However, if his mind has been trained by past experience and he has learned to differentiate between the false and the true, if he is puzzled he can turn to you for the truth of any matter.

An individual's personality is centered about his ability to relate to others. If he relates poorly he's either disliked or ignored, but if he relates well he is considered a pleasant likeable person. What factors account for the various types of personality, and where do they originate? From the moment of birth a baby is learning to relate. The contacts with nurses and parents at the hospital, and with parents and family at home set the stage for a child's learning to relate. For the very young infant, quiet play with your fingers or rocking and singing is both relaxing and reassuring. When he is older—at nine or ten months—he'll enjoy peek-a-boo or pat-a-cake for a few minutes.

In play the idea really is not to amuse the baby but rather to help him grow in understanding through exploration of actions and things, and to help him develop his personality through a satisfying relationship. He enjoys your nearness and attention as he feels your approval and love while you have fun together. Such play fosters affection and intellectual growth as it lays the foundation for creativity, sociability and a warm, giving personality.

We recognize that a basic need of humans is a feeling of self-worth. Young children gain this "good" feeling about themselves from our actions to them. Certainly a parent's role is not to approve of every action of the child, but the youngster needs to know that, regardless of what he does, the parent always loves and respects him even though certain acts are unacceptable.

Courtesy and respect are the oils which lubricate the machinery of human relationship. A sincere compliment for the achievement of another, recognition and concern not only for relatives, friends and acquaintances, but for the welfare of humans everywhere are qualities which are too often ignored by today's youth.

What do you do when a child doesn't show consideration and respect? There are no hard and fast rules for each situation is different. Obviously for your own and the child's good, as well as for the welfare of the family, rudeness and lack of consideration for others should not be tolerated. You can safely allow a child to disagree and to express his feelings so long as he's not abusive and rude.

We expect some differences of opinion between parent and child. Desirable attitudes acquired in early childhood may prevent disaster later in life. A child should know there are consequences for certain acts; for example, he must pay a penalty for taking something that belongs to someone else, or for being inconsiderate or rude to another. The penalty may be the disappointment of a parent, deprivation of an enjoyable activity or whatever means of discipline is most effective with each particular child.

At times parents are discouraged. They wonder what will happen when the child discovers that many people outside his family do not regard as important the moral principles he's taught to live by. We can only hope the home training coupled with a good parental relationship will help him deal successfully with such contradictions and that he will incorporate into himself a large part of the values which the family feel strongly about.

Some psychologists believe morality can be taught.* The technique to use, they say, is moral discussion which centers on moral decisions, how one should act in difficult situations, and why. Such discussions sharpen a child's thinking about right and wrong.

If your child sees children teasing a younger child he may join in the cruel pastime unless he recognizes how the victim feels. Have a discussion with him and try to have him express his feelings about the incident so that you can determine the quality of his moral judgment.

You cannot deliberately teach moral judgment as you'd teach academic facts, but you can stimulate your child's thinking by occasionally raising questions about difficult moral decisions and getting the child to express his opinions. You attempt to keep the discussion going by asking questions without supplying answers, but which eventually lead the child to be dissatisfied with his stage of thinking.

By raising hypothetical cases in your discussions the child is less emotionally involved since he isn't defending himself—and you're not upset. As a result he will feel free to express opinions and together you can talk about them. You can get such discussions started by saying, "What would you do if —?" Pose questions suitable to the child's age and maturity. Choose a time when both of you are calm and relaxed—at the dinner table, just before bedtime, when you're riding in the car or going for a walk.

It is better to have discussions involving moral judgment before the child has done something wrong. You likely will notice signs of approaching difficulty. For example, your four- or five-year-old reveals temptation as he stands before the toy cars in the supermarket.

*Readers' Digest, October 1970, "Teach Your Child To Behave Morally" by Maya Pines.

He has many such cars and you've already told him that this is not a "toy day." He lingers. As you turn, urging him to hurry, you notice he is loosening a car from the card. You're convinced he intends to slip the car into his pocket. After helping him replace it, you move on without a reprimand.

At home when you're both relaxed you might pose a question such as, "What do you think a boy might do if he was alone in a toy store and the toy man stayed in the back room a long time?" Then listen. Allow the discussion to run freely and do not be shocked if he says the boy would take the car and leave before the man returned. Perhaps you've had no previous need to discuss this moral decision with the child and your adult expectations may be unrealistic. All children from all cultures, the privileged as well as the underprivileged, go through the same moral stages though some advance more rapidly than others, and some stop at an early stage. Perhaps many of those who stop were not given the opportunity for family discussions.

When discussions go well you will see results within a few months. Generally families that encourage children to express their opinions and who listen without necessarily agreeing, tend to produce youngsters with a high degree of morality.

You can use the discussion technique for moral training by posing hypothetical cases involving any type of moral judgment you deem necessary. Attitudes and judgments regarding honesty, truthfulness, courtesy, kindness, sharing, consideration for others, prejudice—the list is endless. It is rewarding to discover that as you open up new aspects of moral issues to your child, and as you encourage him to stretch his mind toward his best thinking, he will grow in the important human virtue of moral judgment.

In this "enlightened" age society is rife with intolerant prejudicial attitudes toward minority groups. Prejudice has deep roots in history and culture so that few individuals are free of prejudiced attitudes toward groups other than their own. Our vocabulary is filled with derogatory terms and expressions which reveal discrimination. The old refrain that "Sticks and stones can break my bones but names can never hurt me," is false. There are few children whose psychological armor is so strong that they are not wounded by unkind words, let alone a steady flow of discriminatory actions. For children of victimized groups the result is diminished self-esteem, and too often a withdrawal within themselves or into their minority group.

Prejudiced beliefs tend to bring about the conditions assumed by those beliefs. An unhappy, taunted minority child too often performs as is expected of him by the majority group. Why? Because unconsciously he views himself with the same low esteem with which he is judged by the dominant group.

We verbally deplore prejudice of any kind. *Verbally,* that is, but within all of us there is a varying degree of prejudice. And what effect does this have on the malleable minds of our youngsters? We need pursue the thought no further for we're back to the powerful effect of parental example upon a child's opinions.

If we are to teach our children values which they can live by in adult life we have to help them realize that as we have an ever increasing population, the decisions of one person may affect the others. They need to have concern first for the family, then the community, followed by the nation, and eventually for the welfare of the peoples of the world. Whatever combination of methods we use to train children for social adjustment and intellectual success, the most effective is the way in which we live daily with our children— parental example. The experiences of today shape the character of tomorrow.

Perhaps we sound a little paranoid, but it's true, we're being watched by our children.

Chapter 6
A Guide For Home Training

Now is the time for learning. Whether your child is one week, one month or one or more years of age you cannot go back to retrace the steps in his learning, but you can start today to take him forward. Since children, parents and situations differ, there are no scientific rules which will guarantee learning. There are, however, general suggestions which parents and teachers have found to be effective in guiding children so that their natural curiosity is stimulated.

Children, like adults, resent the authoritarian approach. While there are no shortcuts or pat prescriptions, there is one element which all effective methods of teaching share. That element is sincerity, and it alone will win children. They learn early in life to size us up. If we try to put on a front they see our pretense. Yet they respond when we have the courage to be ourselves with all our shortcomings. Admitting our faults and mistakes is the best way to win our children's confidence. They will usually accept our experience and skill if we are humble enough not to flaunt them. A good parent-child relationship requires mutual respect and trust. When parents treat a child with dignity and kindness they are more likely to induce him to accept desired regulations. Kindness combined with firmness is the basis for a stable relationship.

As you teach your child through the use of the planned and tested activities found in this book, remind yourself that pressure can result in loss of interest and poor work habits. When the child shows weariness or boredom with an activity, you have a clue that something is amiss. Ask yourself these questions: Is the exercise too advanced for the child's mental or physical development? Have you encouraged him to work for too long a time? Is he tired or physically unwell? When his interest wanes, terminate the activity before he becomes discouraged. If the exercise is suitable to his stage of development it is likely that at another time he will enjoy success.

Have you discovered the value of humor when a situation is tense or unpleasant? Try it. Good-natured laughter can easily be invoked, sometimes by a mere inflection of the voice. Laugh *with* your child but never *at* him. Nothing is gained when a child is humiliated, but much may be lost. Punishment also has no value in motivating a child to learn for it amounts to pressure from without himself. To learn, he must be motivated from within.

Two other ineffective methods of inducing learning are overprotection and indulgence. These traits in a parent are entirely opposite of severity, humiliation and punishment, so why are they ineffective? They do not work because they deprive a child of the necessary experience of discovering his ability to overcome difficulties and to take care of himself. Instead, he learns to depend upon others, which discourages independent thinking.

Children must have encouragement if they are to maintain interest. It is easy to criticize harshly, ("You know better than that! Why don't you think?") but such tactics do not result in correction of the problem, for a child seldom changes behavior patterns which have been the object of harsh criticism. Deficiencies are not eliminated by being over-emphasized. Telling a youngster that he can do better, that he would be "such a nice child if only —", means to him that he is not nice and that it is his fault he's doing poorly. Do you wonder that he loses interest?

There are various methods of encouraging a child but words which are effective with one youngster may dishearten another. You need to constantly be alert for the effect upon your child of the comments you make relative to his success or the lack of it. The difference between encouragement and discouragement is subtle. We may discourage one child by expecting too little of him and we may dishearten another by expecting too much. The decision of "too little" or "too much" lies with the individual child, and by his reaction you'll know whether or not your approach is appropriate.

Encouragement depends upon underlying attitudes—your own and the child's—more than upon concrete actions. It is not so much what you do and say as how you do it. Your attitude should be directed toward increasing the child's belief in himself. Discouragement, resentment, and feelings of frustration do not entirely result from external conditions, but from your child's feelings of his own ability to meet them. Point up his areas of strength, and above all, let him know you love him as he is. When you see the good in him and have faith in him he can have faith in himself.

Praise is necessary but it must be used wisely or it may lead to a dependency upon constant approval. Some children become insecure and frightened at the prospect of being unable to meet the expectations of parents. It is important that the child realize that he has value as a person, and that you recognize his value regardless of what he is doing at the moment, even if he fails. This attitude on your part will not cause him to neglect projects or stop his efforts, but it encourages him to keep trying to do his best. And what more can we ask than that he do his best?

You, the parent, have an advantage over the elementary classroom teacher. For as you teach your child he can move ahead at his own rate, free from competition, and with no necessity to show results or to be graded. Neither you or the child should feel pressure to cover material or to do activities which do not meet needs, or which are too difficult for his physical or mental stage of development. Try to keep in mind that your attitude influences that of the child toward enjoyment of an activity; when you approach a project with enthusiasm your attitude is contagious and the child is fired with your pleasure.

Children need to acquire "inner controls." They gain in self-control from parents' patient guidance, encouragement and deserved praise. A quiet comment such as, "Your room looks very neat with everything put away," can be an effective reward for the chore of picking up toys. You'll need to constantly think of new approaches to a special problem. Perhaps on another day a suggestion that it would be fun to "surprise Daddy with a neat room," might be effective; or, "When your room is straightened we'll go for a walk." With this type of guidance your child gradually gains the inner controls to willingly perform necessary duties and he is rewarded by a feeling of pleasure at having done a good job. And his pleasure is doubled by the knowledge of his parents' pleasure in his success.

And how do you feel? You have the warm inner glow that comes with the knowledge that you have been successful in stimulating your child to move one step closer to the acquisition of the inner controls so necessary in a well-adjusted, contented person. And you realize that the democratic, friendly approach to new learning which includes shared responsibility, is a more effective method of gaining a child's interest and cooperation than is the autocratic approach with the sharp voice employing faultfinding, pressure, criticism and punishment.

Listening is an important two-way factor in learning. It is as necessary that parents listen to their child as that he listens to them. Facial expressions tell a child just how interested you are in what he is saying. Courtesy needs to be stressed so that children are aware that they are impolite when they unnecessarily interrupt someone who is talking. Let your child know that you value good listening habits by such comments as, "I enjoy reading to you because you're a good listener."

A child's success in school is dependent upon his ability to listen. If you can help your youngster to gain good listening skills you'll be instrumental in giving him a tool which will be helpful to him during his entire life. Later in this book you'll find numerous activities which were designed to train a child to listen effectively.

For too long society has failed to develop in children a healthy respect for the dignity of work. Children need to be introduced to the world of work at an early age. Postponing such orientation until a child is in secondary school can put him at a disadvantage. You can point out and discuss types of work in both the trade and professional areas. Gradually the child will come to have respect for useful work and an awareness that responsible citizens are able to satisfy their basic needs through profitable work.

As a child is exposed to the various types of work he will learn about his own interests, which may stimulate him to thinking about his future. Though few children in adulthood will follow through on their childish preference for a type of work, they learn from the experience for they've accepted as a certainty the fact that as an adult, they will work.

Nearly all children possess some creativity which may be increased by encouragement and training. It also may be dulled by certain child-rearing and teaching practices. The creative talent needs to be encouraged from early infancy, but it increases at about age three and reaches a peak between four and four and one-half. Sometimes it drops when a child enters kindergarten, perhaps because of teachers' and classmates' pressure to conform.

The creative child has an intense curiosity. He asks constant questions and enjoys testing and experimenting. He is usually sensitive to what he sees, hears, touches and experiences. He often finds unexpected uses for ordinary objects or gives uncommon answers to questions. He is likely to try tasks too difficult for him, but rather than being frustrated by his failures, he accepts them as a challenge. His attention span may be longer than usual for his age.

Creative expression comes from within. Encourage this inclination, for if you ignore or ridicule it, or treat his questions as unimportant, the child may stop asking them. Creative free-thinking adults did not grow in a vacuum, but in an environment which encouraged creativity. Children's imagination grows when they live in a home which exposes them to a variety of experiences where they can work with many kinds of materials, and where they can experience success and failure as they work on challenging projects.

When your child is small you'll need to help him in finding ideas. With time you'll see him working more creatively as he thinks of new problems which challenge solution. Encourage him to look for the unusual or uncommon, for this trains him to observe, and when he sees something unusual, to question why.

There are two sources of creative motivation, namely internal and external. When a child is young, by providing motivation toward creative projects parents are "priming the pump" in the hope that eventually he will be pushed by an inner urge to attempt new projects on his own. The traits of personality which determine our inner drives are acquired early in life when they become fairly well fixed, so that later they manifest themselves as habits of our inner thoughts and actions.

When your child has completed a project, however crude it may appear by adult standards, your reaction to what he has produced should be positive, else he soon will hesitate to try new ideas. Standards are important but they must not be too rigid, for when a child is beginning to carry out independent ideas he needs a feeling that he has been successful. Conformity to rules can stifle creative ideas. You may make suggestions to encourage your youngster to use materials but he should be turned loose to follow his own imaginative ideas.

Try to see that the child has a quiet time and place to work on his projects. Don't interrupt him while he's working, even to give praise, for the interruption might come at the instant he was about to make a creative discovery. And attempt to motivate him to complete projects and to follow through on his ideas. Sometimes leading questions will encourage a child. Questions such as, "How are you going to finish your yellow house?" or, "You have put your toys away very nicely. Can you hang your clothes up so your whole room will look neat?" Positive suggestions may gently nudge him to complete an activity.

Creative efforts often are messy. Without stifling his creativity you can safely have rules for cleaning up and limits about places to paint or display collections.

Most preschoolers enjoy making up stories, and this is a normal stage of development. When your youngster creates a fantastic tale, please don't tell him he's lying. You might say something like, "You have a good imagination to think up a 'pretend' story like that." Such comments help him to make the distinction between fantasy and reality. After reading a story to him you might ask, "Do you think this is a true or a pretend story? Why?"

Teaching a child to think creatively requires creative thinking on your part. A good rule to keep in mind is, "Nudge, don't nag!" And gently nudging a child into intellectually profitable activities is a challenge. When he asks, "What is there to do?" you could suggest that he think of three things he might do. Just thinking of possibilities will occupy his mind and he is more than likely to hit upon one that appeals to him.

Creative thinking also may be used in teaching your child to solve problems or to perform tasks he dislikes. You might, for example, suggest that he think of ways to straighten his room more easily. Don't interrupt his flow of ideas, no matter how unlikely, lest you discourage him. Eventaully, after discussing possibilities including doing the work immediately after breakfast, or leaving it until a certain day, he may hit upon the solution of hanging up clothes when he takes them off and putting toys and games away when he finishes with them so that he never has a large disagreeable cleaning job facing him.

Talk to your youngster about your own creative efforts. The room you are decorating, the color of the accessories, the way you plant your flowers and shrubs in the yard, and when you're buying clothes, the reason for attempting to visualize new clothing with the old accessories.

By encouraging your child to think creatively you are likely to have a youngster who is more content, for he can see not only what is, but what might be, and this is one of the chief traits that distinguish humans from one another. It appears that restlessness arises from the disuse of our aptitudes as though our talents are craving outlets and development and when we dam them up they torment us to be loosened. For this reason parents do their children a great service when they encourage creative imagination in solving the problems of living. Gradually children learn that by forcefully pushing restlessness and anxiety from mind there is room for creative ideas which lead to interesting activities. And this practice promotes greater intellectual development.

You can encourage your child's artistic talent in many ways. When you're making cookies let him suggest shapes instead of using the regular cookie cutter. When you go to an art museum, don't make fun of the abstracts and say you don't know what they're supposed to be; instead, talk about shapes and colors and ask the child what he likes about the painting. Encourage him to make decorations for the house, and *do* put them up. Trust yourself and your child to do "crazy" things. You'll be pleasantly surprised with the results.

Depending upon the age of the child, an activity which requires creativity is telling stories. As he tells his story you might write it for him and suggest that he make illustrations. Art activities are helpful in relieving tension or in working off strong emotions as well as being an area which gives a child the chance to be different and to express his individuality. When he shows you a project he is working on, instead of asking, "What is it?", have him talk about it and tell you what it is. Be careful not to be concerned about perfection, and don't yield to temptation to "touch up" your child's projects or you may destroy his satisfaction with his efforts and cause him to feel the project is not entirely his.

Art not only is therapy which enables a person to express emotions, feelings and thoughts, but it develops skills in the use of various techniques, tools and materials as it strengthens reasoning skills. In creating an art project a child is called upon to reason and to make decisions regarding the best way to express his thoughts and ideas.

In the event you or your child sometimes feel stymied by creative projects, conformity art may be helpful. This type of work calls for little initiative on the part of yourself or the child. Types of conformity art which may occasionally be used are: (1) Pattern art in which patterns or designs are colored or cut out. (2) Outline art. Stencils are traced and the picture is colored or cut out. (3) Copy work. A picture is shown and the child copies it. (4) Dictation art. You give directions which the child follows step by step.

While conformity art can be fun, too many experiences of this kind can destroy a child's urge to express his individuality, and though talent in art and high intelligence are not positively related, art is an activity which most children find relaxing and enjoyable, and one which they use often when encouraged.

Start early in your child's life to teach him to solve problems and to think critically. Discuss with him situations which have importance. Present, for example, such questions as, "If you became separated from me in a large crowd, what would you do?" His solution requires critical, creative thinking. With guidance you can lead him step by step until he becomes aware that everything he sees and hears on TV and from playmates is not necessarily true. As he grows older he needs to know there are various points of view on almost any topic, politics, religion and civil rights, and that he may not agree with some views. Once learned, good problem-solving habits usually will persist.

Most creative, critical-thinking children have a high self-image. They know their capabilities and limitations. They prefer learning by questioning, inquiring, searching, manipulating and experimenting. They are always trying to find out how things work. Their energy seems almost limitless.

The test of intelligence is not what we know how to do, but how we behave when we don't know what to do. Any situation or activity that puts a problem before a child which he solves for himself sharpens his intelligence. The arts, like crafts and skilled trades, are filled with problems, which is why skilled artists and other individuals in creative fields of endeavor are likely to be sharp-witted people.

You will find your child is intrigued by science for it can satisfy his natural curiosity and give stimulation to his inquiring mind as he makes discoveries through observation and experiments.

Do take time to answer his questions. If he asks something of which you're uncertain be quick to say, "I don't know, let's find out." In this way you're teaching him to seek out information which may include a trip to the library. This will start the habit of "looking it up" in reference books such as encyclopedias, atlases, almanacs and dictionaries.

In a child's early years you can lay the foundation for future interest in science at higher levels, for he'll see that science answers questions and solves daily problems. As together you discuss, explain, experiment and research, you're encouraging the child to have an inquiring mind, which simply stated, is good thinking. Together you question what you see and hear, you see differences, classify, understand relationships and draw conclusions on the basis of evidence you've discovered. Science should be viewed as a thrilling study, the door to the unknown.

Most children are naturally curious about the world around them. Life is filled with mysteries which science can explain. Your youngster will have questions about stars, the sun, the moon, about what makes the wind, the difference between rain and snow, why objects fall down on earth and float in space, and dozens of other things. Areas of interest at different stages of development will include time, the adaptation of plants, animals and humans to their environment, conservation and ecology, good health practices and dozens of others.

Simple experiments are an effective method of acquainting a child with scientific principles. As an example, suggest that he plant beans in three paper cups and distribute them in different parts of the house. He will be surprised to see the lack of growth of seeds kept dry and in a dark cold place as contrasted to the ones in the sunlight which were watered regularly. He will be even more surprised to see the small plants bending toward the lighted windows. Such a simple experiment teaches that plants need soil, moisture, warmth and light to grow well.

Teachers recognize the value of experiments in teaching science. You too will help your child to learn the "why" of things by promoting experiments which help him learn something he didn't know before. Keep the experiments simple so that he can see there is no mystery in what is being done. Encourage him to express opinions about what happened. He may wish to do the experiment several times. If he is unable to form an accurate conclusion, and if he is young and his attention span is short, you may choose to explain the "why" of the experiment. But whatever you do in science, as in other areas of learning, keep it fun for the child.

You'll find that science and other areas of interest overlap. Fine! So do they overlap in everyday life. Just follow your child's interest of the moment, and if they engulf many areas before he has formed a conclusion, so much the better.

Most children are ready for introduction to mathematical ideas at an early age. They need to know how old they are and their house and telephone numbers as soon as they are sufficiently mature to retain this knowledge. The point of teaching arithmetic is two-fold; to help children deal with numerical situations which they'll face in life, and to strengthen the powers inherent in the mind.

A young child needs much contact with concrete ideas before he is able to think on an abstract level. He recognizes that two cookies are less than ten cookies when he sees them on a plate, though he likely would not understand if you told him "Ten is more than two." In casual everyday life he needs many such opportunities to think about and to observe mathematical concepts, relying heavily on concrete observations. You can make frequent use of familiar objects when teaching number concepts—objects such as shoes, mittens, candy, cookies, books, etc. A chalkboard and flannelboard also are helpful devices. Avoid talking too much, but instead show him by demonstrating the point you're making with concrete objects. Gradually, as he matures, the concrete objects can be replaced with pictures of the objects. Finally he is able to comprehend the meaning of abstract numbers without the presence of concrete objects or pictures.

With your guidance the child will discover that to make a group of blocks larger, more blocks are added to it, while to make it smaller some blocks are taken away. Thus he is being introduced to the concepts of addition and subtraction. He also needs concepts of more or less, thick or thin, narrow or wide, long or short, heavy, part of, faster than, and as much as, for these concepts pave the way to later arithmetic learning.

Your child will absorb knowledge from your conversation with him and other family members of other meaningful arithmetic terms including up and down, above and below, high and low, on top, middle and bottom. In numbers he becomes aware of few or many, as many as, more than, not as many as, none, some, all, everyone, more or less. In size he soon understands the meaning of big and little, large and small, and short and long. He needs to recognize the common colors of red, blue, yellow, green, brown and black, and later he recognizes purple and orange.

Parents hear much discussion about the "New Math" and many are frustrated at being unable to help their children with simple problems. Relax. The facts we parents learned as children still are true and useful. Your child will learn what we did, and in addition he'll have the opportunity to discover new things.

New mathematics is a way of teaching old established facts, as well as new ones, in such a way that a child understands why they are true. If he understands basic mathematical principles he will be able to apply them to situations he encounters later in life. New mathematics teaches children to learn by discovery rather than by memorization. You are teaching new math when you give your child two cookies and then place one more beside the two. He discovers that there are three cookies and that 2 + 1 = 3. In the same way if he eats two cookies, he discovers that 3 − 2 = 1. You have introduced the addition and subtraction concepts and the child has made a discovery about numbers.

Mathematics can be meaningful, exciting and fun. To a child it is like playing a game, but like all games he needs to know the correct terms. Because the terminology used in math today sometimes sounds strange to us, parents feel frustrated. Keep in mind as you read the following terms that the basic facts are unchanged.

Terminology of Modern Math

1. *Sets.* A set is a related group of objects. The dishes in the cupboard are a set, the various vegetables in the refrigerator drawer are a set, as is the silverware in the drawer. A set might be made up of objects we wear, (shoes, hat, coat, dress) of things we eat, (meat, potatoes, vegetables, milk) etc. Soon it will become natural for you and your child to call a group of related objects a set.

2. *Equivalent Sets.* If you have an equal number of objects in each of two sets, you have equivalent sets. (Three balls and three dolls are equivalent sets.) The child will easily absorb the meaning of the term through your explanation.

3. *Numbers and Numerals.*
"Number" means how many.
Examples: 4 objects in this set.

   1 object in this set.

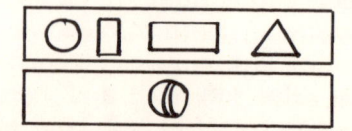

"Numerals" are the symbols used to name the number.
Examples: When there are two objects we write the numeral 2.
   When there is one object we write the numeral 1.

4. *Number Line.* Your child understands the meaning of the word "line." Extend his understanding to include a number line which is a straight line connecting two points, and which is divided into equal spaces that are named by numerals. It begins with 0, meaning "not any."

```
0   1   2   3   4   5   6   7
|---|---|---|---|---|---|---|
```

Show the child that by starting at 0 and moving to the right, you get *more*. This is addition. To add 2 and 3 have him place his finger on 0 and move as many spaces as the first numeral (2). The second numeral in the problem (3) tells him to move his finger three more spaces. This brings his finger to 5, and tells him that 2 spaces and 3 spaces are 5 spaces. He has solved the problem and discovered the answer for himself.

He can also use the number line to understand the subtraction concept. To subtract he makes the number less than it was before. Example: $5 - 3$. He places his finger on the numeral 5 and moves his finger *backward* (to the left) three spaces. He finds there are only two spaces left. Then, $5 - 3 = 2$.

In closing our discussion of mathematics we must emphasize that words mean very little to young children. You'll find the effective way to communicate mathematical ideas is by means of "things" rather than words. Show, don't tell. By using this method the child gradually will build a solid foundation for his later years of mathematics.

Your child will learn to read as the result of daily experiences. His name on gifts and in books, on stop signs and ads on TV all teach reading. He reads long before you give him a book to read but these daily experiences whet his appetite for reading. The stories you read to him, the example set by parents who enjoy reading and by his natural inclination to imitate people he loves as well as by curiosity about the printed word and a desire to conquer it, all are positives working for you as you provide planned experiences to lead him toward the reading process. Reading readiness includes physical as well as mental readiness. A child's development in all areas, physical, mental, and social have a definite effect upon his academic success.

About five percent of America's children suffer from reading difficulties. Reading habits, it is believed, start in infancy. Being stimulated visually soon after birth is related to a child's fascination with reading materials that is essential if he is to read well and to enjoy reading. One reason for our belief that early visual stimulation is necessary to good reading habits is illustrated by the fact that prematurely born children who are confined to the sterile surroundings of the incubator for the early weeks or months of life often develop reading difficulties in school. We assume part of the problem may be early deprivation of visually stimulating surroundings.*

Though much research remains to be done in the reading area no one will deny that an adequate reading ability is a great asset in today's life. Reading is a complicated process involving the use of symbols (letters). Because of varying individual rates of physical and mental development, your child may be ready to read earlier or later than youngsters of acquaintances.

In approaching the exercises in the Reading Section of Chapter Seven your attitude should be one of "This is fun." If you don't sense a pleasurable response in the child, you'd better back off to an easier or different type of activity.

The growth pattern of a child seldom is uniform. He may learn rapidly in one area, but at a slower pace in another. There is no best way to teach reading to all children because of individual differences. Since you cannot know which approach will be most helpful to your child you should be willing to experiment and to be flexible, ingenious, and creative in leading him to an enjoyment of reading. Keep in mind that nothing must happen which would cause him to approach learning with a fear of failure, for his attitude toward learning to read is of greater importance than his rate of progress.

When a child has an emotional upset or is physically not up to par you should forego attempts to work on reading activities. At such times don't risk "turning him off on reading," but instead use a light, creative art activity.

To be successful in reading a child needs to acquire ways of identifying new words. "Sounding it out" is essential to independent reading. Many activities are included in the exercises which will lay the foundation for him to unlock the pronounciation of words.

Many preschool children will read informally, with the parents' guidance, without actually using a pre-primer reading book. This is fine. Don't feel the necessity to have your youngster read from a book unless he shows definite readiness and is eager for "book reading." When you're convinced he's ready, choose an attractive pre-primer with few words and many pictures.

Before giving a child a new book to read it is advisable to teach him words and sentences he'll meet early in the pre-primer. Use blackboard and flannelgraph exercises to teach the words he'll find in the first story. There should be only a few. When you're confident that he'll meet with success, give him the new book. Holding a book

*Teachers' Voice, January 11, 1971

as he reads is a new experience for a child who has previously read only signs, words and a few sentences. At first about all he can be expected to do is to get the words out. Recognition of words requires great concentration and is an achievement. As he becomes more accustomed to reading he'll read more smoothly and gradually will begin to use expression and to comprehend what he's reading.

Encourage the child to read with his eyes without pointing with his finger. You can prevent the common practice of following the line with a finger by giving the child a liner or marker. A liner is a strip of paper approximately six inches by one inch which the child places below the line as he reads, sliding it down line by line as he reads the page. But watch out! Some children will even use the corner of the marker to point to individual words. If he insists on pointing, explain that this practice slows up his speed in reading since his eyes can see several words at a time if he'll allow them to sweep across the line, but that by pointing at one word, he limits his glance. Another common practice which slows the eye span during silent reading is lip movement as a child whispers the words. To control this tendency, suggest that he hold a finger over his lips to keep them closed.

What do you do about the word which your child cannot read? When he is beginning to read it is better to tell him immediately. If necessary, tell him the same word several times. If he continues to have trouble suggest that he look for clues such as "Can you read the rest of the sentence or look at the picture and decide what the word might be?" Soon he'll enjoy using his knowledge of phonics as he "sounds it out, then says it fast."

However, the most difficult words likely will be ones which cannot be pictured or sounded out, such as is, was, were, those, they, who, what, etc. The more bothersome words are the ones you should concentrate on in word games and exercises.

Before reading a story it is best if you previously teach the new words so that when your child meets them in the story he will recognize them. This practice is followed by classroom teachers, and you'd do well to do the same since the youngster then is likely to read the new material easily. There is no better motivation to learning than success.

When a child reads fluently on an early first grade level he will enjoy "reading for fun." Fun reading should have a high interest level and it must be easy reading with few new words. Ask the librarian or your child's teacher, if he is in school, to suggest appropriate books to encourage independent reading.

For a child to learn most effectively criticism, correction and commands should be kept to a minimum. When you're tempted to arbitrarily say "No," try to consider the child's request in the light of its importance. Unless there is a good reason for a negative answer, perhaps you should reconsider. Do look at your child's good qualities and let him know you admire them. By showing him that you respect his right to think for himself, his respect for your opinion will grow.

At the risk of being repetitive we must say again that nothing will be gained by negative teaching. We need to point out children's successes, not their failures. A child who has experienced frequent success has a strong self-image and is better equipped to cope with occasional failure. Do approach your child's learning with positive feelings for his chance of success. Don't make him stick to a learning task when he doesn't want to. His interests and responses are your best guide to his readiness for learning. If you observe this guide you'll refrain from undesirable "pushing."

Eliminate cutting expressions and the words "wrong" and "mistake" from your conversation with the child. Try to form questions in such a way that he has a good chance for success. If he fails, make a comment such as, "That was a hard question. After we talk a little more, you'll understand." Then proceed to reteach without comments about his not listening or thinking. Try always to use constructive rather than destructive criticism. Accentuate the positive whenever possible. And when he appears tired or loses interest, stop immediately, for pressure will produce anxiety in both the child and you.

And when your youngster starts kindergarten, if he has an attitude of anticipation toward academic and social learning you have given him a foundation upon which to build his future education and his life.

The exercises, activities and games which follow in Chapter Seven are designed only as your guide. Follow your own ideas in adapting them to your child's needs and allow him to use his creative ability in varying them and in producing new learning experiences.

Happy teaching!

Chapter 7
Activities, Exercises and Games Which Promote Learning

This chapter of 225 tested activities, exercises and games, together with dozens of variations and suggestions, is designed to promote learning as children are entertained.

The numerals preceding the activities denote only the order in which they appear. The chapter is divided into sections. The exercises in each section are arranged in the order of difficulty with the easier activities first, while the more difficult ones appear at the end of the section.

Activities Which Interest The Infant .... Exercises 1— 22

Toys Which Promote Learning .... Exercise 23

Perceptual (Sensory) Experiences For
   The Older Child (3 to 8 Years) .... Exercises 24— 42

Coordination .... Exercises 43— 53

Listening .... Exercises 54— 69

Communication And Language .... Exercises 70— 79

Art .... Exercises 80— 84

Creativity................................ Exercises 85— 90

Science .... Exercises 91—109

Social Behavior .... Exercises 110—130

Reading and Phonics .... Exercises 131—178

Arithmetic............................... Exercises 179—214

General Knowledge .... Exercises 215—225

Activities Which Interest The Infant

The objectives of the tested activities for infants are directed toward stimulating the curiosity and providing experiences which encourage learning through the sensory approach—the visual, auditory, and tactile senses as well as by knowledge received through sensations of taste and smell.

Some babies develop quickly, some go slowly. Most infants learn unevenly, sometimes with plateaus or even backtracking at times, then racing ahead by leaps and spurts. Attempt to use the activities and exercises with your baby to which he gives attention and exhibits enjoyment. He will then learn at his own rate.

1. *The Child's Room*
Decorate the baby's room in a bright color which will give a cheerful, gay atmosphere. Bright pictures on the wall add a pleasant note. Use an attractive picture-colored bumper to line the crib. It's a good idea to move the crib about the room periodically to vary the child's view.

2. *Keep Baby With You*
To help the baby learn to relate to you, as well as for him to see and hear new things, you can carry him about from room to room as you encourage him to look at objects in the house. Talk to him as you show him a bright picture, a pretty lamp or the family pet.

When you're busy in the kitchen put him in a safe place where he can watch you work. When he can hold his head up, a canvas sling that holds him to your hip permits you to occasionally carry him about while leaving your hands free. He gains much information by going about with you as you do housework.

An inclined infants' seat gives baby a wide view of activities in the home, and is preferable to being isolated deep down in the crib or buggy during waking hours.

3. *When Baby Is Lonely*
If he's restless when you're not with your child the gentle sound of a small clock ticking next to the crib, or of a radio or record playing soft music may be sufficient to comfort him. A wind chime near the window where the wind can catch it is especially soothing to a small baby.

4. *Talk To Baby*
　　To lay the foundation for language and to teach him to relate, you should talk to your baby from the first time you hold him. Talk to him when you greet him in the morning, when you feed and change him and put him to bed, as well as when you go about your housework and he watches. Soon he will try to communicate with you by varying his crying to tell you when he's hungry, tired, bored, or hurt. In a short time he'll be babbling and experimenting with sounds.
　　Listen to him, and when he stops, talk to him. Soon he'll get the idea of what verbal communication is all about. As a rule, it is better to avoid baby talk because your infant needs a model to learn correct language.

5. *Music*
　　Babies enjoy musical tones. Sing to your youngster. Sing songs you enjoy as well as nursery rhymes and children's songs. Sing while you rock him and when you're happy, and sing as you work. Baby will absorb your relaxed, cheerful attitude.
　　Play records often, records which you enjoy and also children's records.

6. *Naming Objects*
　　You can give your child informal training in language and early preparation for talking by directing his attention to different objects and naming them as you change, bathe, feed or work near him. A child given such training usually understands and talks earlier than he otherwise might.

7. *Encourage Baby To Touch*
　　Allow your baby to have many tactile experiences. The softness and feel of a pet's fur, a bird's feathers, a velvet ribbon, the smoothness of the satin binding on his blanket, the coldness of linoleum and the warmth of carpeting, the roughness of a terry towel, the softness of mother's hair and the sharpness of father's whiskers before he shaves, the feel of sponge rubber, tissue paper and newspapers—all of these touching experiences teach the baby about the world around him. Later on as his brain calls for information, he will rely more on seeing than touching, but even as a two- or three-year-old he will feel the need to touch new objects.

8. *Allow Baby Physical Freedom*
　　To encourage development of the muscles as well as the mind

give baby as much freedom from play pens, cribs and confining clothing as is consistent with safety. During waking hours he may lie on a pad on the floor where he has plenty of room to move arms and legs freely. If you put him on his stomach on a hard surface he'll soon surprise you by learning to turn over.

9. *School Begins At Two Weeks*

A baby can develop his potential much sooner than it formerly was thought possible if he is encouraged to be confident and inquisitive early in life. Training is possible through the use of homemade devices and toys as well as by excellent commercial sets available in the infant sections of department and toy stores.

You can train your baby's eyes to focus and to follow a moving object. Such activity stimulates his interest and curiosity.

Suggestions:

a. Hold a brightly colored object before the baby's eyes at a distance of about 7½ inches, which is the usual distance for focusing on a moving target in the early days of life. Move the object slowly as the baby's eyes focus and track. Follow various movements with the object so that the eyes follow large and small, vertical, horizontal and circular movements. Vary the objects color, size, shape and pattern for the baby's increased attention and enjoyment over the time span of several weeks.

Suggestions for brightly colored objects which will attract an infant's attention include construction paper circles, squares and triangles, concentric circles (revolve them slowly), diagonal stripes and balloons.

b. Use the brightly colored objects described in the above exercise. As your child's ability increases, vary the distance of the object from close to the eyes (7½ inches) to as far as baby's eyes continue to follow. Repeat the motion several times, varying from left to right and high to low in relation to the baby's eye level.

c. From five weeks of age to six or eight months babies enjoy stabiles or mobiles. You can easily make these simple training devices by tying various brightly colored objects to a wide elastic band or a wooden pole which can be suspended above the crib and adjusted to varying distances from the baby's eyes. These devices can be made using such available objects as a small mirror, a stuffed toy, rattles, plastic blocks, etc.

By three months many infants who have had adequate eye stimulation readily grasp objects within their reach.

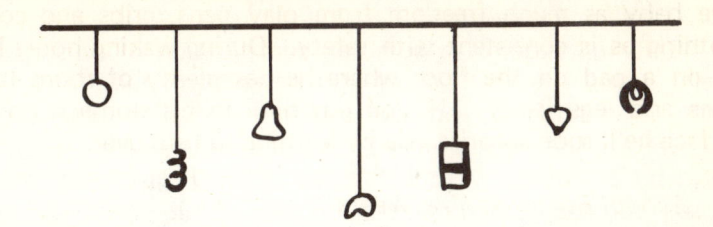

d. Attach several bright-colored light-weight objects to a wire coat hanger with varying lengths of string to create a mobile. Balance the objects so that they hang evenly. Suspend the mobile from a light fixture or hang it near an open window or door, or you can use a fan to create a current of air. Baby will enjoy watching the dancing movements of the objects.

Light-weight objects which may be used in making mobiles include large feathers, balsa wood gliders, paper birds, butterflies or insects.

e. When baby is restless he may enjoy watching a lighted lamp, or you might set a few colored glass bottles or jars in the window so the sun shines through them.

10. *Motor Activity*

To provide training in motor activity when the infant is three to six months of age you can fasten a balloon or a rubber toy animal to the crib with a piece of elastic. Soon he will learn to strike or pull on the objects and will enjoy thier action as he releases them.

11. *Peek-A-Boo*

The old game of peek-a-boo will help the baby to tolerate a brief separation from you as well as to provide him with a play period as he develops coordination of hand muscles in the grasping and pulling of the handkerchief.

Cover the baby's face loosely with a large handkerchief or other light-weight cloth. When the child is ready he will grasp and pull the cloth from his eyes as you exclaim, "Peek-a-boo!"

12. *Listening Activities*

Stimulate your baby's curiosity by encouraging him to listen to sounds about the home. The tick of a watch, the sound of the door bell, the hum of the vacuum sweeper, the rush of the spin cycle of the washer, the splash of running water and the beep, beep of the telephone busy signal will teach him to be aware of sounds about him. As he listens, tell him what the sound is that he is hearing.

13. *Crawling Experience*
   Crawling requires a complex coordination of sensory stimuli. There is evidence that babies who never crawl may later have difficulty in learning to read due to lack of adequate visual perception and eye muscle development acquired as the child explores his world by crawling. Most babies will crawl if given the freedom to do so. Constant confinement to crib or play pen can seriously impede a child's development.
   Suggestions:
   a. Place the baby on the floor in a safe "baby-proofed" room. To encourage crawling put favorite toys just out of his reach.
   b. Give the infant the opportunity to crawl on tile or linoleum as well as on wooden floors and carpeting. Each type of floor sends varying stimuli to the baby's growing brain.
   c. When the weather is suitable and you can supervise him, allow baby to crawl outdoors on the grass.
   d. Have a shelf of toys or a low toy box near the baby so that he can crawl to it and choose items of interest.

14. *Word And Object Association*
   You can encourage your baby to associate words with objects though he isn't yet able to form words by naming objects he is looking at or playing with. (Kitty, bread, car, book, etc.) Continue talking to him. Show him you're pleased when he babbles an answer. Talk to him when you work about the house and when you drive in the car or shop at the supermarket. ("We'll get some milk and some cheese. You can hold the can of peas.") And remember to use correct English, keeping baby talk to a minimum.

15. *Reading To Baby*
   You can instill an enjoyment of books in a child at an early age. By the time your baby is ten months old you should be reading to him from children's books containing large pictures of familiar objects and animals. Encourage him to look at the pictures and to help you turn the pages. Some excellent books contain fur-like animals and other devices involving the sense of touch. Baby will enjoy feeling of them.
   Keep story time a brief pleasure-filled period for both yourself and the baby. Though he won't understand every word, he'll associate reading with enjoyment.
   Include nursery rhymes and jingles in your reading as baby will find pleasure in the rhythm and rhyme.

16. *Musical Rhythm*
    Clap your hands in time to the beat of music. Occasionally grasp the baby's hands and gently clap them to the beat of musical records. He'll enjoy the activity as he feels the rhythm of the music.

17. *Hide And Seek Games*
    You can help your infant form concepts about the permanence of objects or persons not immediately within his sight. At first you may need to "hide" objects while he's watching, then ask him to find them. He'll laugh and show pleasure at locating them. Soon he'll learn to search when he hasn't seen you hide them. Later, when he shows readiness, the game may proceed to regular hide-and-seek as you hide from one another.

18. *Trips Outside The Home*
    New experiences result in intellectual growth so try to give your youngster many brief trips outside the home.
    Suggestions:
    a. Your child will be interested in visiting other children near his age, and though he isn't old enough to play with them, he will observe the other child as they play in the same room, but with different toys.
    b. Take your toddler for short walks. Encourage him to look at birds, trees, flowers and insects. Try to bring stimuli to his mind from many of the senses. Have him smell the rose, feel the velvety softness of the petals and the sharpness of the thorns, see the beautiful bright color of the blossom and hear the buzz of nearby insects.
    On longer trips, or when he becomes tired, your child would find his stroller most acceptable. At other times he'd enjoy pushing it for a short distance.
    c. In winter a child can tolerate a short time outdoors, even on a cold day. A healthy youngster can gain much knowledge from a few minutes spent with his parent in a blowing snow storm. The feel of the snow splashing his face, the howl of the wind, the sight of snow flying "crossways" rather than drifting slowly to the ground, the sharpness of freezing air striking his lungs and the strange feeling when the sides of his nostrils temporarily stick together—these sensations can be times of learning for a child.
    d. Trips to the supermarket can bombard your toddler with sensory stimuli. He can see the brilliant colors of the fruit and vegetable counter, feel the coldness of a carton of ice cream,

and the softness of a loaf of bread as he hears the clang of the cash register. He can smell the fruity odor of fresh pineapple, and if he becomes restless, he can taste the smooth mellowness of a ripe banana. None of this will take more of your time than it would to insist that he "sit still and be good."

19. *Continue Talking To Your Child*
To help the child acquire a speaking vocabulary and to increase his understanding of words you'll verbalize your thoughts and impressions. When he is speaking a few words you are encouraged to talk to him as you go about your housework. The more language he hears the greater will be his vocabulary when he begins speaking freely somewhere around his second birthday.

20. *Playing Games*
You can teach the child to follow directions if you ask him to carry out simple directions such as, "Please bring me your shoe." When he understands and complies, reward him with a hug.
Play "games" which involve pointing to parts of the body. "Point to your eyes. Point to your nose." Continue with ears, feet, toes, hands, fingers, thumb, elbow, knee, hair, etc.

21. *Continue Reading To Your Child*
To increase the youngster's vocabulary and knowledge and to further enjoyment of books you'll continue reading to him. Favorite rhymes and simple stories he'll enjoy over and over. Inexpensive books are available in drug stores, supermarkets and book stores. The toddler age is not too early to take him to the library where you can help him select a book, and where he'll see you and other children and adults choosing books.

22. *Records And Radio*
Your child can receive excellent auditory learning and stimulation from listening to children's records and folk music. Background music consisting of classical selections or musical comedy songs often prove restful to a tired child, while at the same time he learns to appreciate good music.

Toys

23. You can further the development of your child's mentality and provide training in muscular coordination through the use of objects which he can touch, taste, grasp, throw, shake and bang. The

following toys are helpful between the age of three and eighteen months.

    Small stuffed and sponge toys
    Plastic blocks
    Floating animals and toys for the bath
    An unbreakable mirror
    Metal pie pans
    Cardboard boxes
    Smooth, non-sharp metal cans
    Sponge rubber ball
    Spools, four or five on a string

    Expensive toys are unnecessary. A baby will have fun and learn as he places a block in a coffee can, fits together a set of plastic bowls, puts blocks into a shoe box, and endless numbers of other inexpensive and accessible items which are found about the house.

    By the time a child is one to one and a half years he needs toys and activities which encourage experimentation, such as the following:

    a. Toys and objects which teach in and out, inside and outside, on top and on the bottom, larger and smaller, little and big, etc.

    b. Nesting blocks, cups, bowls, barrels and boxes and cans with lids.

    c. Wooden or plastic rings that fit around a central core.

    d. Wooden or plastic blocks which may be used to make trains, houses or towers.

    e. Simple wooden or plastic puzzle-form boards with a few pieces which fit into the form. (Squares, circles, triangles or rectangles, or pieces painted to represent fruit.)

    f. Make a mailbox by cutting a slot in a cardboard box and let your toddler play mail man by depositing old letters in the slot.

    g. Allow your young child to climb stairs. If you have none, his father can build a sturdy three step set which will fascinate the baby as it teaches physical coordination. (Commercial sets are available at most toy stores.)

    h. Children love to play in the water, either in a shallow plastic pool or in the bathtub. They'll pour, splash, float toys and squeeze sponges with enjoyment. (At this age water play must be closely supervised.)

    By age three a child will still enjoy many of his toys from earlier months of life, but in addition he needs toys which prepare him for life outside the home. There is an intellectual component in all areas of play. You'll find your child learns more by experimenting and exploring than he does from your lecturing.

Toys that a three- to eight-year-old will prefer may be:
a. Toys that trigger the imagination. Puppets, blocks, sand, paper and crayons and paints.
b. Toys which allow the child to pretend he's grown up. Housekeeping toys, nurse and doctor kits, farm sets and animals, machinery, trucks, trains, planes, and various types of dolls.
c. Toys to love. Stuffed, soft, cuddly animals.
d. Action toys. Climbing bars, slide, sled, rocking horse, all types of balls, tricycle, wagon, cars, swings, and climbing activities—in fact, all types of riding, pushing, pulling, climbing, putting together and taking apart, rearranging and grouping, and throwing activities—any of these which are safe for the age range and maturity of your child will help him to learn and progress mentally, physically and socially.
e. Some toys foster intellectual learning and will provide a child with hours of fun. Such toys are: Nesting blocks, magnifying glass, flashlight, boxes, large-pieced inlaid puzzles of wood or masonite, take-apart toys, a large magnet, various types of counting toys and number puzzles, rhythm instruments, record player and records, farm buildings and animals and machines, and simple games—these toys require thinking, stimulate the curiosity and can lead to new learning experiences with your guidance.

Sensory Experiences For The Three- To Eight-Year-Old

Children become aware of the world by way of the senses. They learn by seeing, hearing, touching, smelling and tasting. Because perception plays an important part in a child's rate of learning, you might find it helpful to reread Chapter Four, pages 14 through 20, "How Children Learn."

The exercises in this section are planned to stimulate learning via the sensory approach.

24. *"Seeing" Without Eyes*
Young children love to feel things and to explore with their hands. This activity stimulates the senses other than sight.
Suggestions:
a. Put a few objects in a paper bag. Blindfold the child and ask him to choose something from the "mystery bag." Ask him to explore it fully, to feel, smell, listen, and perhaps to taste it.

In the beginning objects should be easy to identify. An orange, a crayon or a cookie should be quickly recognized.

Gradually the child can identify more difficult objects—stuffed animals, favorite toys, a cap or an empty dish. Eventually you may wish to test him on various types of food such as pudding, cheese, fruit and different kinds of meat.

b. Hide several familiar toys in a paper bag. Ask the child to reach inside and to identify the toys by touch. Vary the game by telling him to find specific toys.

c. You can make a book of learning experiences for your child. To make the book, use a notebook with loose-leaf rings and the cardboard that laundries put in men's shirts for the pages. Punch holes for the rings. Look through your sewing box, cabinets and drawers for materials that will teach your preschooler as he feels them. A piece of cotton will feel soft to his touch, and soon he'll learn the word cotton. A section of an old leather belt will teach him of the material used for shoes and purses. A length of string will remind him of wrapping packages, fishing or flying kites. Sandpaper feels scratchy, while wax paper is soft and shiny. Buttons, leaves, toothpicks, tissue paper, aluminum foil and similar items may be glued to the pages.

With your help the child will learn associations by touch as well as sight. Eventually he'll enjoy the book by himself as he identifies the materials by touch alone.

d. Matching by sound will interest a child. Fill pairs of small bottles or boxes with different substances such as sand, salt, gravel, small rocks or rice. Ask the child to shake them and to find the pairs by sound.

25. *Learning And Using Colors*

There are a variety of ways to teach color words to your toddler. In conversation say such things as, "Get your red ball. Your new shirt is blue. Do you want to wear the yellow or the green shirt?"

You might suggest that he arrange his toys by color, as, "Find all the red blocks and put them together." (Continue with other colors.) The child might string wooden beads, placing the beads of one color together.

If you casually include color words in conversation the child will soon recognize the primary colors.

26. *Matching Colors*

a. Cut 3 by 5 pieces of construction paper in half. Ask the child to find the mates. A two- or three-year-old can match three or four colors. As he becomes skilled add new colors until he can match as many colors as you provide.

Vary the activity by asking him to find two reds, two blues, etc.

b. When a child is learning colors a set of color dominoes is an entertaining and valuable teaching aid. You can make the set as follows:

Cut 3 by 5 pieces of construction paper in half, using the more common colors of red, blue, green, brown, black, orange and yellow. Paste two colors side by side on a 3 by 5 filing card to make a color domino. Make a "double" of each color. (Two halves of the same color.) Make many combinations of colors so that in all you have approximately 28 dominoes.

Play the game as in regular dominoes. Turn dominoes face down. Each player draws seven and keeps them concealed from his opponent. The person who has a double leads and his opponent matches the color. (Yellow on yellow, etc.) The first player now matches either the first domino played (the double), or the end of the second domino.

Continue play, alternating players until one person plays his last domino. He is the winner.

In the event a player has no match, he may draw from the center of the table until he draws one which matches, and play continues.

27. *Jigsaw Puzzle*

Select an appealing picture from a magazine and cut it into pieces, the size depending upon your child's maturity. Have him place the pieces in proper position to make the picture, after which he may paste them on cardboard to reconstruct the original picture.

28. *Foreground And Background*

Look at pictures in storybooks and magazines. Ask the child to tell which objects are nearby and which are far away.

29. *Copy The Design*

Pegboards are excellent learning devices. Buy two small pegboards. Set up a simple design with pegs on one which the child is to match on the other board. As he becomes more skilled you can increase the details and difficulty of the design.

30. *Learning Shapes*

A child can be taught to recognize shapes (circle, square, triangle and rectangle) by cutting several of each shape from paper. Vary the sizes so that you have several of each shape. Ask the child to put all the circles together, all the triangles, the squares and the rectangles. Call the shapes by name as you talk.

Another way to teach observation as well as shapes is to have the child look for geometric shapes in home furnishings, designs in clothing and in buildings. Example: "How many rectangles can you see in the living room?" (TV, door, window, pictures, table top, etc.)

31. *Word Games*

Word games teach observation and give training in visual and auditory perception. You'll think of many variations to the following examples. You might say to the child:

a. "I'm thinking of something in the room that is green. What is it?" Concentrate on teaching one color at a time. When the child is reasonably sure of that color, continue with another, but include the ones previously taught in review. Use color words often in conversation. ("Would you like to buy the green ball or the red one?")

b. Shapes and sizes may be used in word games. You might say, "I'm thinking of something in your toy box that is round. What is it?" (Ball.) Include triangular, rectangular and square shapes, teaching each one thoroughly before proceeding to the next shape.

When the child is ready, combine the concepts of color, shape and size in one question. "I'm thinking of something in the kitchen that is white, rectangular in shape and larger than the dishwasher. What is it?" (Refrigerator.)

32. *Right And Left*

You can teach the concepts of right and left through casual conversation, as:

a. "We'll put your right arm in the jacket first, then your left one," or, "This is your right shoe, now we'll put on the left one." Occasionally ask the child to point to his right or left hand or foot so that you can determine whether or not he is grasping the concept.

Other suggestions for teaching right and left include asking the child to find his left (or right) mitten, and when you read to him, point out that we read from left to right across the line. You'll become aware of numerous opportunities for teaching right and left.

b. Direct your youngster to locate a "surprise." (Candy, a new book, etc.) To prolong the game you may include "detours" in the road to the surprise.

Example:
   Go ten steps to the right of the fireplace, turn left five steps, walk straight ahead to the dining room door, turn right six steps, etc., etc., until the game ends at the surprise.
   c. Try to "catch" the youngster with directions such as: Touch your left ear with your right hand. Touch your left eye with your left hand. Touch your right foot with your left hand. Touch your right knee with your right hand.
   When an error is made, the players change roles until the second player makes an error. (The leader should "call" the error.)

33. *Observe As You Drive*
   A child will learn to be observant if you encourage him to watch for specific things as you drive. For example, "See how many red cars you can count." Vary your directions to hold his interest by including many different things such as yellow trucks, orange school busses, out-of-state licenses, a specific make of car, etc.

34. *Observation And Recall*
   Show the child a picture from a magazine or book. Suggest that he study it closely for details and general impressions. Remove the picture and ask him to tell you what he saw in the picture. You might ask questions such as, "What were the people doing? Why? What toys did the children have?" Try to lead him to recall as many details as possible.

35. *Look And Learn*
   There are many kinds of lines. To teach observation ask your child to look for straight lines, curved lines, jagged lines, broken lines, fat lines, skinny lines, etc. Point out the various types of lines by drawing them on paper. Find examples in home furnishings, in buildings and in pictures. Look for types of lines while walking or driving.

36. *Can You Remember?*
   Ask your youngster to recall as many items as he can from his last trip to the supermarket; to the department store, to the gas station; to the zoo.

37. *Instant Recall*
   Place several objects on a table. Ask the child to look closely at them for one minute. Put the objects in a bag and direct the youngster to ask for as many as he can recall. Place them on the table as

he names them.
> *Variation:*
> After the child has studied the objects, ask him to close his eyes while you take one item away. See if he can recall which object you removed.

38. *Recalling Objects In Order*
Arrange from three to six objects on the table in a line. You might use toys, books, silverware, dishes or crayons. Direct the child to watch and listen as you point to and name the objects from left to right. Ask him to look hard at the objects and the order in which they are placed, and to try to remember. Allow him to concentrate for one minute. Remove the items and ask him to name them in the order in which they had been arranged.

Continue the game allowing the child to arrange objects as you recall them.

39. *Similarities And Differences*
The ability to see similarities and differences is readiness training for reading.

> *a.* Cut identical pictures from magazines. (Find two or three from the same month of various magazines.) Ask the child to put the ones that are alike in piles.
>
> *b.* Matching numerals is a good teaching device. Make three or four of several numerals and cut them apart. The child will find the ones that are alike and place them together. He does not need to know the names of the numerals to be successful. He need only be observant. However, before long he will recognize the numerals by name through your conversation during the game. ("You're right. You found three 2's.")
>
> *c.* Matching letters also is good training in seeing likenesses and differences. Print several sets of letters on cardboard, as: A a, B b, C c. Cut them apart so that the capital and corresponding small letter are on the same card. In conversation with the child refer to them by name as "Capital A and small a." Remember the child need not know the letter names to be successful in matching. Be sure that you give him only a few cards, at first, so that he is certain to meet with success. In the beginning, perhaps only six cards with two different letters, such as three A a and three B b cards. As he becomes accustomed to the game you may increase the number of letter cards.
>
> In speaking of the cards, though you call them by name, do not pressure the child to remember the names. However, you

show pleasure when he does so. ("That is an A! You're very smart!")

d. Your child will enjoy matching patterns. You could arrange three to five blocks in a pattern. See if the child can copy the pattern with identical blocks. Increase the number of blocks and the difficulty of the pattern as he shows the ability to progress.

Tinker Toys, Erector set pieces or any set which contains many parts may be formed into patterns which can be copied.

e. To help the child see likenesses and differences you might draw a series of pictures. (Animals, buildings, shapes, toys, fruit.) Make one or more identical to the first picture. Ask the child to underline the figures that are the same as the first one.

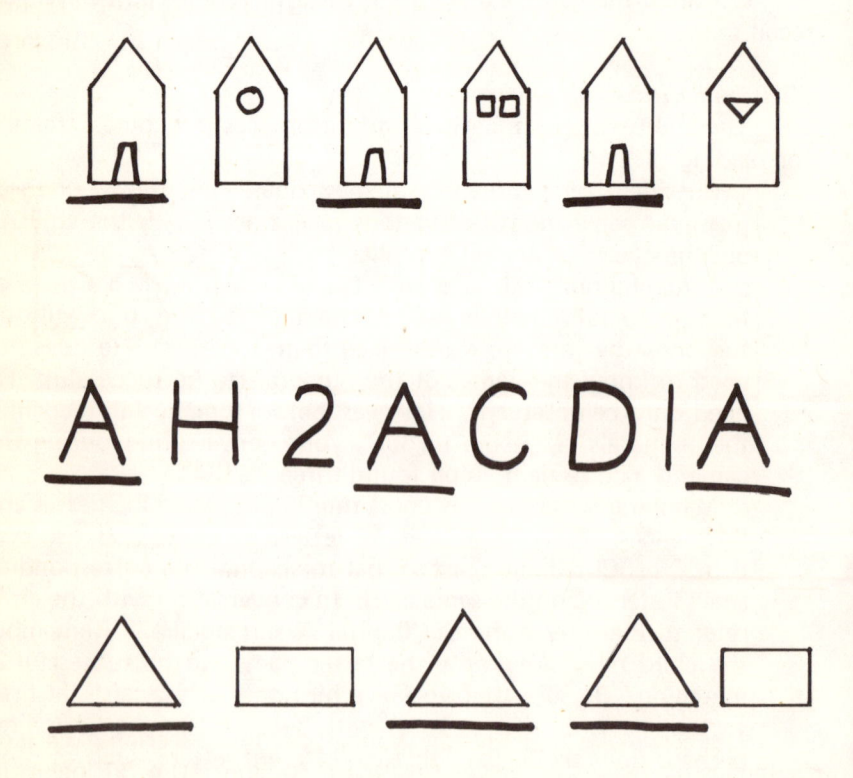

Variation:
Use rows of letters, numbers, or words, again asking the child to find the ones that are different from the first.

40. *Puzzles*
   a. You can make a variety of inexpensive puzzles by pasting magazine pictures to shirt cardboard. When dry, cut the picture into large pieces. As the child becomes more skillful, the pieces may be cut again to increase the difficulty.
   b. Large letters and numerals may be drawn on shirt cardboard and cut into half. Again, depending upon the ability of the child, you'll make the pieces of sufficient size so that he will successfully solve the puzzle. You might use two colors of magic marker, one for letters and one for numerals. As he successfully completes a puzzle, casually mention the names of the symbols he has completed. ("You've made a B and a 3.")
   c. The child will enjoy putting together a cardboard puzzle of his name, and other easily recognized words. (Stop, go.)
   d. Colors too may be taught by the puzzle method. Mount circles of color with the identifying color word on the cardboard before cutting it into two, three or four pieces.

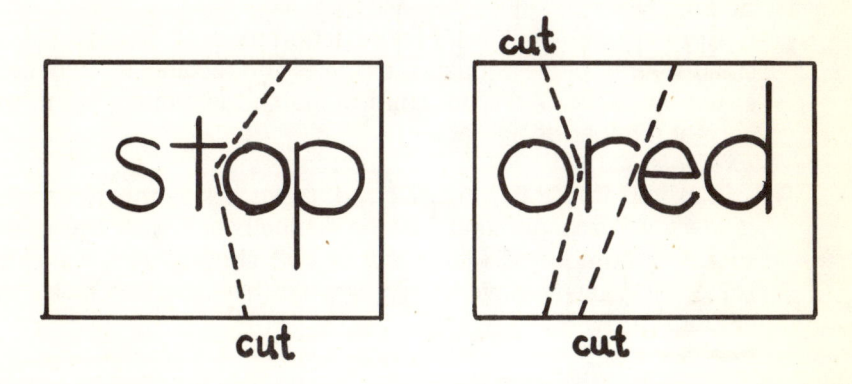

41. *Use A Flannelboard*
   You can make a serviceable flannelboard by covering a piece of wallboard, plywood or heavy cardboard roughly 30 x 30 inches in size with flannel or felt. It is a good idea to have one color on one side and a different color on the reverse side. Sew the two pieces of flannel together in the fashion of a pillow slip and pull the "pillow slip" over the cardboard or plywood board.

Cut out pictures, large numerals, letters, words or sentences, depending upon your plan for their use. Paste a strip of flannel or sandpaper to the back of each one. You'll find the words, pictures, letters or numerals will stick to the flannelboard if they're firmly pressed against it.

Uses for the flannelboard are almost endless. It is an excellent, inexpensive teaching device. Adjust the difficulty of the exercises to the maturity of your child.

Suggestions:

a. Telling a story. Have the child arrange magazine or other pictures in sequence to illustrate an original story which he makes up.

b. Cut large letters, both capital and small sets, from construction paper. Find pictures to match the letter sounds, as: a — airplane, apple; b — boy, baby, barn. Ask the child to match the pictures with the letters and to place them side by side on the flannelboard. (You may need to paste a circle of construction paper on the backs of the pictures so that they will cling to the flannelboard.)

c. Cut large numerals from construction paper, 0 through 9. Cut small figures, circles, squares, triangles and rectangles, from construction paper. Ask your child to match the numerals with the correct number of figures.

Example:

Can you find a 5? Put five red circles beside the numeral 5.

d. Place a large numeral on the flannelboard with the corresponding number of figures (from "c" above). Ask the child to see how many ways he can arrange the figures to make the amount of the numeral at the top.

Example:

Numeral 5 with 5 squares could be arranged to show that:
$0 + 5 = 5$ $1 + 4 = 5$ $2 + 3 = 5$ $3 + 2 = 5$ $4 + 1 = 5$ $5 + 0 = 5$

e. Make word cards using words appropriate to your child's ability. Suggest he say the word and place it on the flannelboard. If he doesn't know the word, tell him, then have him place it in a pile to which he later returns for another trial.

f. Make a few sentences which the child dictates to you. Cut them apart and have him read the sentences to you as he places them on the flannelboard.

g. Teach colors and color words by making circles, squares, triangles and rectangles of colored construction paper. Print the identifying color word. Have the child match the colors to the color words on the flannelboard.

h. Use the flannelboard for addition and subtraction drill in combinations.

Store the materials you've made for the flannelboard in properly labeled envelopes for future use.

42. *Mazes*

Mazes provide visual training and challenge a child's interest. Do not make them too difficult. Let him have the pleasure of finding the work "cinchy." Follow the line to the treasure.

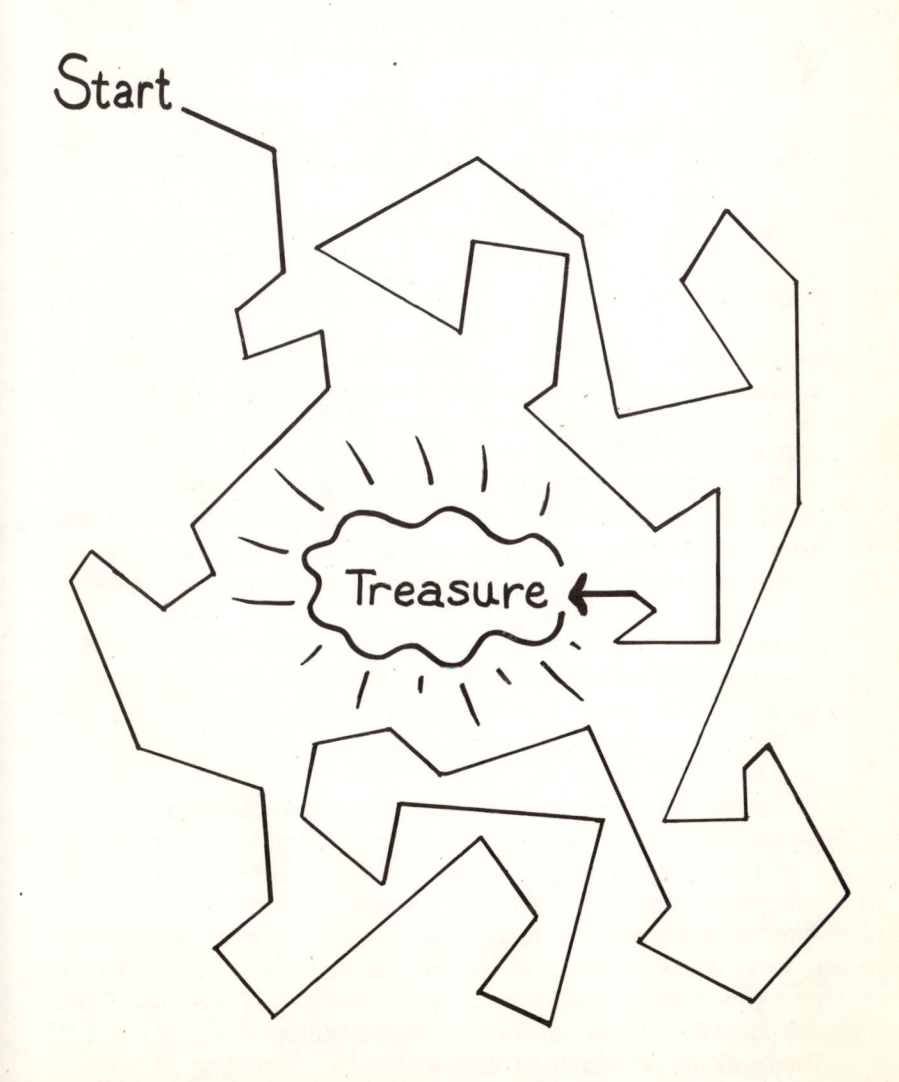

Activities Which Develop Coordination

The success of many of your child's activities depends upon his muscular coordination. The following exercises will benefit him in this area.

43. *Body Size And Shape*
To help the child appreciate his size have him lie down on a large sheet of wrapping paper as you trace around him. He can crayon in his features and clothing and cut out his outline. He likely will wish to tape his picture to the wall. He'll be surprised at his size.

44. *The Carpenter*
Give the child a hammer, nails and a block of fireplace wood or a few small pieces of soft wood boards. He will enjoy learning to drive large-headed nails into the wood, and with practice he will gain in motor coordination. Soon he will wish to nail small pieces of wood together as he builds items dictated by his imagination.

45. *Learning Skills In Dressing*
a. Capitalize on your preschooler's fierce desire to do things for himself by breaking activities into small steps which the child can easily master. Tying shoes, putting clothing on a hanger, washing his face, dressing himself or any of numerous activities children need to learn independently are more easily mastered when broken down into small steps.
Example:
To teach a child to place his coat on a hanger, show him how to spread it open on a bed or table. Next the hanger is inserted into the shoulders and the coat is buttoned. He then carries it to a low clothes rod or hook and hangs it neatly in place.

46. *Learning Methods of Fastening*
To teach your youngster how to fasten his clothing you can make six square eight inch wooden frames. Attach two pieces of cloth to the opposite sides of each frame. He will fasten the cloth together in the center. Design one frame so that the material is buttoned together, another to be snapped, a third to be zipped, the fourth to be buckled and the fifth to be laced and tied. In constructing the tying frame, the tying is simplified if the right-hand tie is of one color and the left one of another color.
Concentrate on teaching one method of fastening at a time.

If you prefer a commercial device for teaching methods of fastening they are available at department and toy stores.

47. *Writing In The Air*
As a readiness exercise for writing, ask your youngster to write large symbols in the air using his finger as a pencil. He may make circles, squares, triangles, rectangles, letters and numerals.

Reverse the procedure and have him write a symbol as you tell what he has written.

48. *Coordination Training*
a. Your child will enjoy playing, "Follow The Trail." You may trail a cord through the house, under the table, over the arm of the sofa, up the stairs, under the bed, back down the stairs, ending at the original starting place.

The child follows the cord, crawling, climbing, and jumping as he explains what he is doing. ("I climbed over the chair, I crawled under the table, I walked up the steps, etc.")

b. Have the child bend forward and clasp his hands in front of his knees to form a ring. Ask him to step through the ring with one foot as he keeps his weight on the other foot, then step through the ring with the second foot.

49. *Motor Skill*
Have the child stand with feet apart, then spring or jump upward and turn either clockwise or counterclockwise as far as possible. When teaching this activity begin with a quarter turn, then a half turn, and as the child's balance improves, he can spin a full turn.

50. *A Trace Race*
On a large piece of paper, using a crayon or magic marker, make patterns as below, about three inches in height.

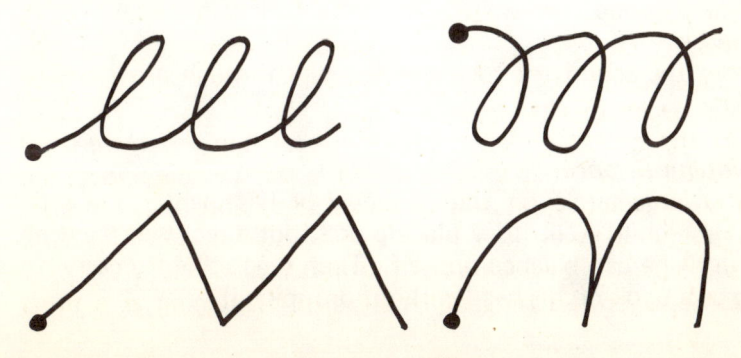

Ask the child to start at the black dot as he traces over the patterns with his index finger, either right or left hand, depending upon his preference, as you count. Tell him to trace slowly so that he goes over all the lines.

After he follows the patterns easily, have a faster race. Ask him to trace each pattern before you can count 15, then 10 and later 5.

When he traces easily have him do letters and numbers with his index finger. Call them by name as you talk to him. ("See if you can trace the three C's before I count 10." Eventually he will want to trace his name and other favorite words.

(See Exercise 53 for instructions for Manuscript Writing.)

51. *Perceptual-Motor Coordination*
a. Place a 2 x 4 about eight or ten feet in length on the floor. Your child will develop visual and motor coordination and perception as he walks the "railroad track." When he does the activity easily, raise the 2 x 4 a few inches off the floor by placing it on two or three blocks for support. Then have him walk the railroad track across the "trestle."

b. Help your child to make gains in eye-hand coordination by encouraging him to try this challenging activity. You can make a large scoop from a gallon size plastic bottle, the kind that bleach and distilled water come in. Cut a portion of the bottle off diagonally, starting with the shoulder of the bottle and removing all of the bottom. A four inch plastic ball or a tennis ball are good sizes for this activity.

There are a variety of activities which may be done with the scoop and a ball, such as:

1) Pick the ball up with the scoop, then throw the ball in the air, catching it in the scoop as it comes down.
2) Place the ball in the scoop. From the scoop, throw the ball into the air attempting to catch it as it comes down.
3) Roll the ball against a wall or building from a hard surface such as a paved driveway. Catch the ball in the scoop as it rolls back.
4) From the scoop try to shoot the ball through a basketball hoop.

52. *Developing Balance*
Draw a large circle on the driveway or basement floor with chalk. Let the child walk it by placing one foot directly in front of the other until he can balance himself. Then suggest he try carrying a bean bag or a book on his head without dropping it.

53. *Manuscript Writing*

Children are interested in learning to write. When your child asks to write his name, or shows interest in making letters, words or numerals, he is ready for this activity. Because young children usually are not well-coordinated, manuscript writing is easy for them to learn since it requires less use of fine hand, arm, eye and body muscles, and is less fatiguing than cursive writing. The letter formations are easily made and consist primarily of simple strokes based upon the use of straight lines and circles.

If your child is left-handed, has especially poor muscular coordination or doesn't grasp new concepts as rapidly as another child, you'll still find that when he is interested in learning to write, he'll be successful, at least in his estimation. Again we repeat, don't press for perfection, and don't hold him for too long a period of time to writing.

As an introduction to manuscript writing, Exercise 47, *Writing In The Air,* is quite beneficial to the young learner. When he asks to write something he "can see," encourage him to use the blackboard in making large letters or numerals, or give him a very large piece of unlined paper and a crayon. When your child enters school, or before, if he seems ready, you may give him lined manuscript paper especially designed for young writers.

If you're to instruct your child in manuscript writing you must be familiar with the principles, else you're hardly prepared to teach him. You can prepare yourself by studying and practicing the following letters. Follow the arrows and numbers.

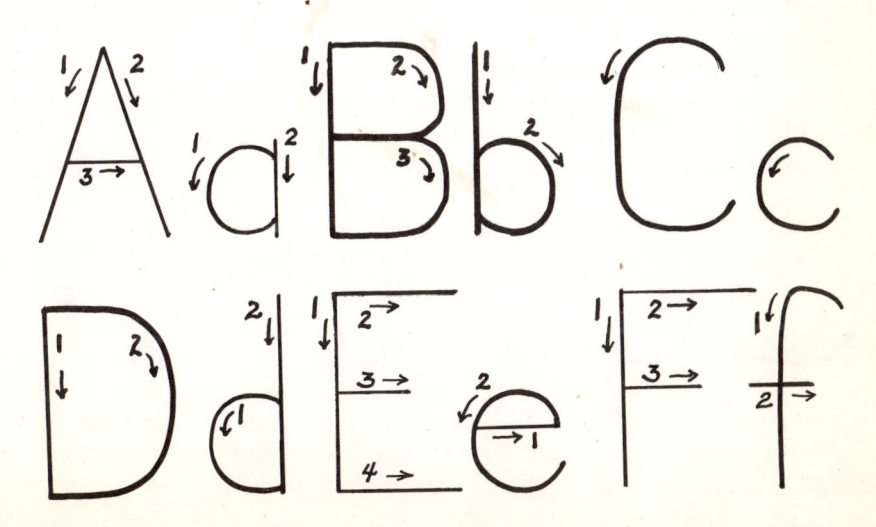

Gg Hh Ii
Jj Kk Ll
Mm Nn Oo
Pp Qq Rr
Ss Tt Uu

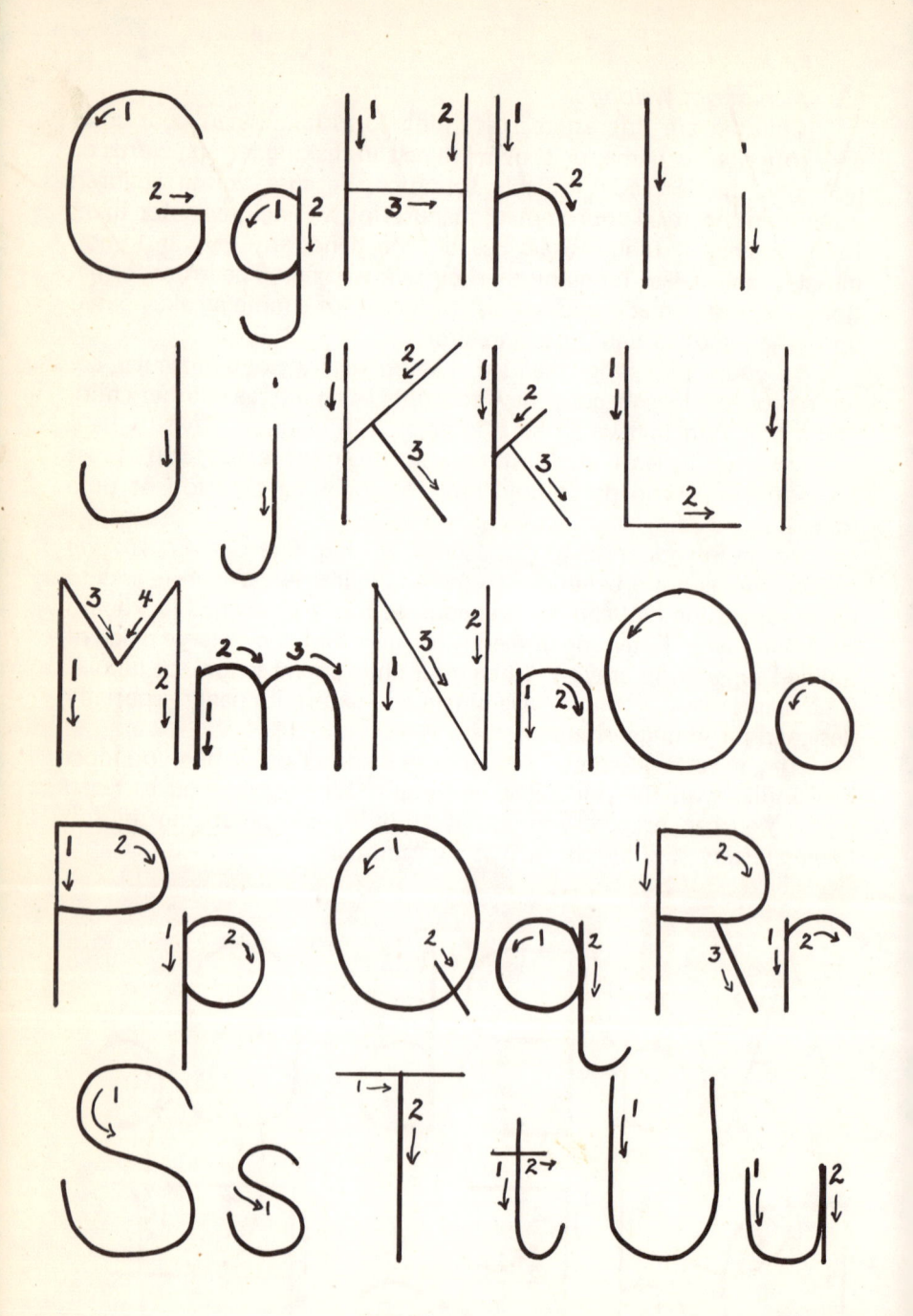

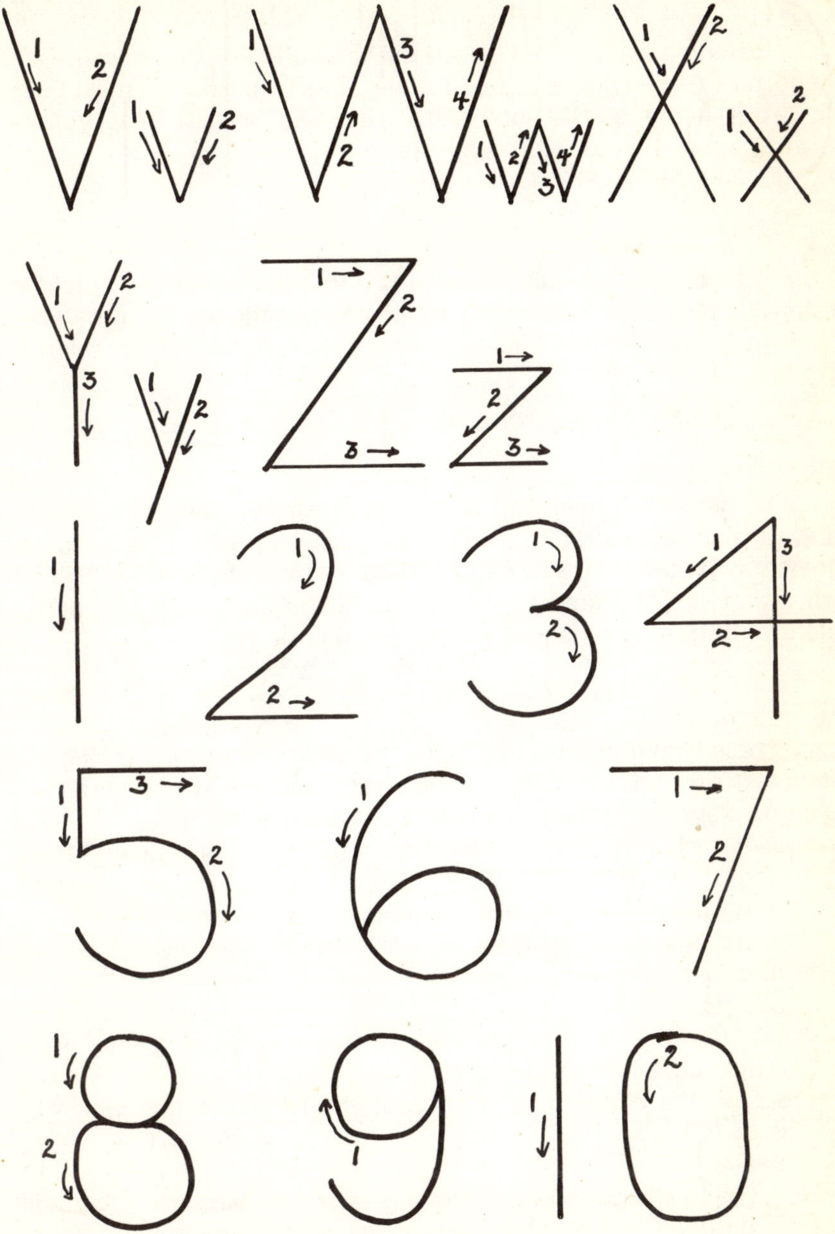

Listening

Listening skills are a necessity in this verbal world. Because it is important that a child is a good listener if he is to gain the most benefit from home and school instruction, we suggest that you re-read Chapter 4, page 15 to page 16.

54. *Following Directions*

With a shoe box and a small toy you can teach your child to listen for directions. Ask your toddler to put the toy in, out, under, over, in front of, behind, above, beneath, and to the right and left of the box.

55. *Draw A Picture*

To determine how well your child listens you might ask him to draw a picture illustrating a story you have read to him. Ask leading questions if he seems puzzled. ("Who was the story about? Show what they did.") Motivate him to do his best work by putting the picture up in a conspicuous place for a day or two.

56. *Sound Games*

These listening games will give the child practice in hearing and identifying sounds and they are good transition activities from a busy exciting playtime to the more quiet meal, bath or bedtime.

a. Suggest that both of you be very quiet as you listen. After a minute ask the child what he heard. (A lawn mower outside, a bird singing, the refrigerator running, a fan humming.)

b. Ask the child to close his eyes and to guess what you are doing to make various sounds.

Examples:

Closing a door, keys jingling, water running, paper being crumpled, a ball bouncing, etc.

c. Ask the child to listen as you whisper a direction which he is to follow.

Example:

Go to the cupboard where the pots and pans are. You will find something in the green sauce pan. (Any small surprise such as gum or candy.)

d. Say, "We will both close our eyes for two minutes. Let's see which of us can hear the most sounds before the time is up."

57. *High And Low Tones*
Play notes on any musical instrument in groups of two or three. Ask which was the highest or lowest tone. Have the youngster stand on tiptoes for very high notes, squat for low notes and stand normally for notes in the average range. This exercise will train him in listening and in distinguishing between high and low tones.

58. *Are You Listening?*
This is an exercise to teach a child to follow directions. Make it a game with the number and the difficulty of the directions appropriate to the maturity of your child. Give the directions only once. In the beginning, and especially with a young child, one direction is sufficient, but as he becomes more skilled the number of directions should be increased. Just be sure that he has more successes than failures, and you will have the correct level of difficulty.
Directions may be given in any area in which a child needs practice, as:
a. "Take your red truck to the toy box." (For a young child.)
b. "Walk to your room, find a story book, close your door, and hop back to me with the book." (For a four-year-old.)
c. "Pick up your toy car with your left hand. Put it on the right end of the kitchen counter. Run it across the counter five times." (For a six-year-old.)
d. "Point to the north with your right hand, spell your name, hop three times on your left foot and sit down on the floor facing south." (For an eight-year-old.)

59. *Sounds*
This exercise, and the variations you'll think of, can be used effectively until your child is in first or second grade. Proceed slowly with new material and play the "games" only so long as the child is interested. When he is able to do so, let him take turns quizzing you. You'll know by his reactions just how well he has mastered the sounds you've taught.
You might say, "I'm thinking of something that starts like **Johnny**. We keep it in the refrigerator. It starts with the "j—j" sound. (Make the sound.) It could be jam, jelly, juice, etc.
When you are teaching ending sounds, you might say, "I'm thinking of something that has the same sound at the end as **ball** and it is round. What is it?" (ball)

60. *Why Listen?*
To help the child recognize the importance of listening, discuss

with him incidents which illustrate the value of being a good listener. Pose hypothetical cases and ask what might happen if the children in the stories failed to listen.

a. Mother planned to be away from home when Jeff returned from school. She told him what he should do until she came home, but Jeff was watching TV.

b. The teacher announced a special animal program was to be given the next day and said there was a ten cent charge. John hoped there would be dogs. When he was home he couldn't remember the day the show was to be, or how much money he needed.

c. The teacher explained how to play a new game. Tim loved to play games but he was thinking about raking leaves with his friend Tom after school.

The teacher called on Tim to be the first leader. He didn't know what to do.

61. *Simon Says*

Two or more people may play this game which sharpens the child's memory and listening ability.

When the game is new, you should be the first leader. Explain and demonstrate that when your directions are preceded by the words, "Simon says," players should do what you do. When your directions are not preceded by "Simon says," they should not follow your directions even though you do the actions. Change leaders after five commands, which may be such as hopping on one foot, skipping, holding up a foot or a hand, winking, nodding, revolving the head, etc.

Praise the child for being a good listener with "sharp ears" when you're unable to catch him after five commands.

62. *Guided Listening*

Teach your child to listen for specific facts. Read a story and ask questions when you've finished. (What color was Jimmy's hair? Was his sister older or younger than he?) If he is unable to answer the questions, reread the story, suggesting that he listen for the specific points in question.

Another method of giving guided listening experiences is to have the child listen to children's records, either poems, stories or vocal musical selections. Ask questions to check listening and comprehension.

63. *Over And Under*
To teach the child to follow directions while using various terms denoting position, ask him to draw a line through the middle of a page of paper. Give directions as:
>Put a circle **above** the line.
>Put a square **below** the line.
>Put a 0 **on** the line.
>Put a 1 **over** the circle.
>Put a 5 **beneath** the circle.
>Put a triangle **above** the line.
>Put a rectangle **below** the line.
>Put a 3 **inside** the rectangle.

64. *Which One Is Different?*
Think of groups of words and ask the youngster to find the one that doesn't belong.
>*a.* Which word doesn't rhyme?

boy	toy	lost	joy
talk	balk	stool	chalk
way	hay	girl	bay

>*b.* Which word doesn't begin the same?

dog	dance	car	doll
baby	bill	bike	pop
child	fire	farm	from

>*c.* Which word doesn't end the same?

cried	walked	singing
thinking	calling	walker
talking	teacher	thinker

65. *Do As I Say*
Tell the child you will give the directions twice for this exercise. Adjust the difficulty of the game to the child's level of ability.
>*Examples:*
>*a.* Print your name on the top line of the paper.
>>Write the numbers 1 to 10 on line 5.
>>Write the alphabet on lines 8 and 9.
>
>*b.* Go to the kitchen and turn on the light. Open the left-hand door under the electric range. Look at the back of the second shelf in the left-hand corner and you'll find something you'll like. Reverse roles as the child gives directions for you to follow.

66. *Following Instructions*
You'll need numerous ideas for teaching the important skill of

following instructions. Try to vary your approach so that the child's interest is maintained.

The following type of exercise demands concentration if the child is to be successful. Don't include too many directions in an exercise.

Divide a sheet of paper into large squares. Give instructions such as:

Write the numeral 2 in the first square of the third row.
Put the numeral 6 in the fourth square of the second row.
Put an A in the last square of the third row.
Put your name in the square just before the A.
Put a triangle in the second square in the second row.

If the child is interested, you can continue until all squares are filled.

You will think of other instructions for developing listening skills if you concentrate on areas in which the child needs practice. With younger children this plan may be used for learning color, shapes, letters, numerals and recognition of sounds.

67. *Can You Catch Me?*

The child listens, attempting to catch you in a mistake, as you make a series of statements, spell words, or give number and nature facts. When you occasionally make an incorrect statement, he challenges you and corrects your mistake.

Examples:
a. A whale is an animal.
Many birds fly north in the fall.
2 and 2 are 4.
2 and 3 are 6.
A sparrow is a bird.
A bat is a bird.

b. As the child progresses and reads fluently, ask him to watch and listen as you read material at his reading level. Occasionally you'll make an error by inserting, leaving out or mispronouncing a word. When he challenges you, ask him to correct your mistakes.

68. *Listening For Sounds*

Read aloud a story or poem. Ask the child to listen for enjoyment and comprehension. Read the same material a second time suggesting that the youngster listen for particular sounds. (Choose sounds which the child has mastered.)

In the following selection you would ask the child to identify words containing w and wh sounds. Show him that if he holds his hand before his mouth when he makes the w sound, he will feel no air on his hand as he will when making the wh sound.

Read the selection slowly as the child listens for the designated sounds.

Wee Willie White went home when his wagon wheel made a whirring noise. Was it broken?

Wee Willie's father was working. He was painting the house white. Wee Willie said, "My wagon wheel whizzes and whirs when it turns."

"Which wheel?" Mr. White asked.

"The back one," Wee Willie said. "The right wheel is the worst."

Mr. White got the oil can. "Your wheels make that whirring noise when they want oil," he said.

69. *How Sharp Are Your Ears?*
Read aloud a few short sentences or paragraphs which contain several clearly stated facts. Tell the child that he should listen very hard since you are going to try to catch him when you finish reading.
Example:

Flies and ants are insects. All fully grown insects have three pairs of legs and three sections to their body. In front is the head. The middle part is the thorax and it has six legs and the wings fastened to it. The back part is called the abdomen.

Ask questions such as:

a. Which two insects were mentioned?
b. How many legs do insects have?
c. To which part of the body are the legs fastened? (Accept "Middle," and say "Yes, the thorax.")
d. How many parts are there to an insect's body?
e. To which part of the body are the wings fastened?
f. Can you remember the other parts of the insect's body?

Communication And Language

Language is a necessary tool to thinking. If your child can put his thoughts into words his communication skills will be sharpened as he learns to clearly and intelligently express his ideas.

70. *Language Training*
Suggestions:
a. Ask the child to choose the best words he knows to describe a beautiful red rose, a storm, the feel of satin, the taste of a crisp

apple, the scent of father's shaving lotion, his feelings when he isn't allowed to stay up late, etc.

b. Give the child ideas which will encourage him to talk. Ask him to tell about a trip he enjoyed, or about what he and a friend played. Encourage him to tell his father and the rest of the family what he did during the day.

c. Ask him to discuss with you the TV programs he enjoys, and during the conversation you'll have the opportunity to point out fact and fantasy. Television can also stimulate his desire for more information about subjects such as animals, the ocean, space and other areas of interest which will lead you to help him find books at the library.

d. Encourage the child's sense of humor. Research shows most gifted children enjoy jokes, riddles, silly rhymes and verbal puzzles. When you join in the fun, he enjoys words and he's learning through language.

71. *Can You Remember?*

This quiet game requires keen listening as it trains the child in memory and expression of his thoughts. Start by saying, "I went to the supermarket. I put a carton of milk in the cart."

The child continues by saying, "I put milk and eggs in the cart."

You then repeat the two items and add a third as, "I put milk, eggs and cheese into the cart." Continue the game as long as the child and you can recall the purchases in the correct order.

At first, two or three items may be as many as the child can recall, but with practice he'll soon extend the list.

Variations:

a. Play the game as above, except that you remove the items from the cart at the checkout counter until the cart is empty.

b. Take items from the toy chest. "I took my red truck from the toy chest," etc.

c. Going for a walk. "I went for a walk and saw a bluebird," etc.

d. Book game. "I took *Peter Rabbit* off the shelf." Then, "I took *Peter Rabbit* and *The Three Pigs* off the shelf." Continue as before until the child no longer can remember the correct order of the books. Finish the game by verbally putting the books back on the shelf in the order in which they were removed.

e. At the zoo. You might start by saying, "When I went to the zoo I saw an elephant." The child continues, "When I went to the zoo I saw an elephant and a monkey." Continue as before.

72 *Tell The Story Of The Picture*

Use any appropriate picture. To encourage the child to be

observant and to look for clues, ask questions as:
- *a.* How can you tell the wind is blowing? (Trees, flowers, clothes and smoke give indication.)
- *b.* Who do you think lives in the house? A family with small children? Teenagers? (Tricycle, dolls, hotrod.)
- *c.* What are the children going to do? Are they happy? Sad? Angry? Give reasons for your answer.
- *d.* What is the building in the distance? Factory? Store? Apartment building? School? How can you tell?

After he has carefully searched for clues in the picture, ask the child to make a story based upon his observation.

73. *The "Adverb" Game*
Suggest that the child think of:
Ways to talk. (Politely, rudely, loudly, softly, pleasantly.)
Ways to walk. (Fast, slowly, quietly, proudly, noisily.)

74. *Communication Skills*
To avoid using overworked words have the child say something in as many ways as he can.
Example:
Can you say, "The bird went away," in other ways? (The bird flew away. The bird hopped away. The bird jumped away. The bird ran away. The bird disappeared.)

75. *Non-Verbal Communication*
Does your child know he can express his thoughts and feelings without saying a word? Tell him you can tell when he's unhappy, though he hasn't told you. Give him time to think how this is possible. Give him hints by sad or happy facial expressions, body posture and hand motions.

Change your facial expressions, and ask him to tell how you're feeling, and what you might be thinking about. By this time he likely will grasp the idea of non-verbal communication.

Reverse the procedure and as he "makes faces," you can guess how he feels or what he's thinking. Try communicating with him silently using only facial expressions and the hands.

76. *Verbal Communication*
Whenever possible give the child the opportunity to express his thoughts and feelings. Encourage him to include new words in his vocabulary. Examples of topics which should lead to verbal exchange are:

a. Discuss ways of getting information. Ask, "If we want to go on a picnic, how can we find out what the weather is likely to be?" He may think of several methods including TV, radio or newspaper. Ask him to pretend he is the weatherman giving the information.

b. Begin a story. Stop at a dramatic point and ask the child to finish it.

Example:

Jean had a pet parakeet which was allowed the freedom of the house. One day when her brother came from outside, the parakeet flew through the door and lighted in a maple tree in the backyard.

What do you think Jean did?

c. Talk about the seasons. Emphasize the present season. If it is fall, discuss signs of fall. Take a walk and look for signs. Upon returning home your child might enjoy making a fall picture. When his father returns from work, have the child tell about his walk and the picture.

Use this plan for study of the remaining seasons, winter, spring and summer, at the proper time.

77. *Opposites*

Direct your child to listen for opposites in each sentence. Some sentences may have more than one set of opposites.

a. More people live in the <u>city</u> than in the <u>country</u>.
b. The forest is a <u>quiet</u> place, but the airport is a <u>noisy</u> one.
c. The baby <u>laughs</u> when she's <u>happy</u> and <u>cries</u> when she's <u>sad</u>.
d. <u>Black</u> and <u>white</u> zebras, <u>big</u> and <u>little</u> lions, <u>young</u> and <u>old</u> giraffes live at the zoo.
e. Mary is <u>tall</u> but her sister is <u>short</u>.
f. Soup is <u>hot</u> but ice cream is <u>cold</u>.
g. We climb <u>up</u> the slide, then we go <u>down</u>.
h. In winter it's <u>cold</u> <u>outside,</u> but <u>inside</u> the house it's <u>warm</u>.
i. You <u>ask</u> a question and I'll <u>answer</u> it.
j. When the <u>boys</u> <u>came</u> <u>in,</u> the <u>girls</u> <u>went</u> <u>out</u>.

78. *Sentence Stories*

A different approach to sentence structure is to place a list of letters at the top of the child's blackboard or paper. Suggest that he make a sentence so that, according to the order of the letters, he has a word which begins with each letter. There can be no wrong stories if the sentences are complete. The child may need help with spelling.

Examples:
B m a h r   Bill made a home run. Or, Betty's mother ate her radish.
T t i y   The truck is yellow. Or, The tree is young.

79. *Completing Stories*
To help your child think creatively as well as to give practice in spelling and writing you might prepare the following type of exercise and ask your youngster to fill the blanks to make a story.

It was a dark night. I felt _____ . I was walking to the store when I saw _____ . I began to _____. Suddenly I saw Mr. _____ .
  I called, "_____."
  He said, "_____."
  I told Mother of my adventure. She said, "_____."

Art

80. *Craft Materials Stimulate Creativity*
Craft supplies need not be expensive. Children love to experiment with various materials and are pleased with their creations. We offer only a few suggestions, you'll think of many more. You likely have most of the following materials suggested in these exercises.

a. Crayons and water color paints. Encourage the child to express himself through original pictures, and to tell about his picture. Do not ask him, "What is it?" If you're not sure, you might say, "Tell me about your picture."

b. Old sheets may be cut up and crayoned to make costumes or linens for the doll house. The colors will last longer if you place wax paper over the crayoned design and press it with a medium hot iron.

c. Plastic and lace doilies can be used for making Easter bonnets or for clothes for small dolls.

d. A package each of white manila and assorted colored construction paper will be used for art projects and for many activities and exercises.

e. Finger paint can be made by using laundry starch and food coloring. Make the starch quite thick, according to directions on the box, and add food coloring.

Interesting designs may be made by using a comb, sponge, an old hair roller or paint brush, instead of the fingers. After the painting is dry the child may like to experiment with adding another color on top of the first.

If only a small amount of finger paint is needed, mix food coloring with a spoonful of hand lotion or a daub of toothpaste.

White shelf paper moistened with a sponge makes a good paper for fingerpainting projects.

f. Long lengths of unused wallpaper can be used for murals. If the child wants plain paper, use the back of the strip.

g. Draw with wet colored chalk on damp construction paper or newspaper. When the drawing is dry, spray lightly with hair spray to preserve it.

h. White paper plates may be crayon decorated and made into clocks by adding numerals and hands, or a picture may be made by pasting an attractive scene or flower in the center of the plate and the outside will serve as a frame.

i. Your youngster will find many uses for a box of odds and ends—bits of ribbon, cloth, brightly colored paper, old greeting cards, seals, stickers, magazine pictures, foil wrapping paper and string. With only a bottle of glue and scissors he can cut, paste, and arrange original designs and greeting cards.

j. All children like sculpturing with clay. You can buy clay at a hobby shop or prepare your own by mixing two parts of salt to four parts of flour and gradually adding water to the right consistency for easy handling. Food color or powdered paints mixed in will give the desired colors.

Have the child try new tools for variation in sculpturing. Pencils, a toy rolling pin, fork tines, and cookie cutters give variety to the appearance of clay projects.

The clay mixture may be used to make attractive Christmas tree ornaments. Have the child work on a wax paper surface. He can shape the ornaments with cookie cutters. Don't make the shapes too thick or they'll crack. While the clay is still moist, insert Christmas tree hooks, or make a hole with a straw so colored yarn may later be inserted for a hanger. Place the ornaments on an ungreased cookie sheet and bake in a 350 degree oven from one to two hours, depending on the thickness. When the ornaments are cold, they may be decorated with poster paint. When thoroughly dry, shellac them and you'll have ornaments that will last indefinitely.

You and the child will think of many projects which will be unique using the above clay mixture. Baking them slowly in the oven makes the objects more permanent.

k. Poster paints are used for variety in color. They're also inexpensive. Sometimes instead of a paint brush, the child will enjoy creating new effects by using an old toothbrush, a sponge, a crumpled wad of paper towel or a piece of yarn.

l. When crayons are broken into small pieces have the child grate them onto a piece of white paper. (Use a kitchen grater.) Cover this with wax paper and iron it to melt the wax of the grated crayons. Very pretty wrapping paper may be made in this way.

m. Translucent designs and pictures can be made by arranging bits of bright tissue paper on a piece of wax paper. Add crayon shavings and pieces of colored string or yarn. Cover with a second sheet of wax paper and press with a warm iron.

81. *"Magic" Paper*

On a gray day when your child is restless and not in the mood for more serious projects, give him some carbon paper and let him trace pictures from magazines or coloring books.

He may enjoy making his own carbon paper in a variety of colors. Suggest that he choose a crayon and that he heavily color an entire sheet of plain white paper, which he can use as carbon paper. Ask him why carbon paper makes "magic" pictures.

82. *Decorating Trees*

Fasten a branch about three feet high in a container of sand. The child will enjoy decorating his tree for various seasons and holidays. (Spring, summer, fall, winter, Christmas, Valentine's Day, Easter.)

Ornaments may be made from clay (see exercise 80, project J), aluminum foil, foil pans, construction paper, folded tissue paper, painted macaroni which is strung, etc. When decorating the branch for spring, summer or fall, either paper or real leaves may be used.

83. *An Easy Art Project*

Give the child an assortment of scrap materials such as bobby pins, screws, nuts, bolts, beads, yarn, small pencils—anything at all that is not too large. With Elmer's Glue have him fasten the objects in a haphazard manner to an old plate, cigar box or a piece of wood. Glue them closely together so that very little of the foundation shows through. When dry, spray with gold or silver paint.

You may follow this plan using shell macaroni, beans, or any reasonably small material instead of scrap. Attractive projects may be created in this manner.

84. *Self-Serve Paper*
So that the child always will have a supply of available paper, install a small cafe curtain rod to be used as a roller for a large roll of white shelf paper, on the wall of his room. This practice will save you time when he wishes to draw or cut paper. Keep his crayons and scissors nearby and he'll be challenged to try ideas as they come to his mind.

Use your child's colorful designs and artwork for gift wrappings. He will be pleased, and so will relatives and friends who receive the unique packages.

Creativity

Creativity and art are closely related, as are all areas of life that require imaginative thinking. If we can allow children to solve problems with originality, we are encouraging them to think creatively. Reread Chapter Six, pages 32-35 on creativity.

85. *Enjoyment of Music*
Provide your preschooler with simple musical instruments, rhythm sticks, xylophone, drums, etc. An inexpensive phonograph which he can operate and a few children's records will give him hours of enjoyment and will lay the foundation for future music appreciation.

Continue singing to him and encourage him to sing with you. Soon he'll sing favorite songs alone.

If you have a piano or other musical instrument you can stimulate the child's imagination by playing a low, deep note slowly and regularly in a walking rhythm. Ask him what animal the rhythm sounds like. Hopefully he'll think of a large lumbering animal such as the elephant. Play a high note with a rapid rhythm. This might be a mouse running or a bird hopping.

86. *Let's Pretend*
   a. Have the child pretend he is a cat, duck, dog, lion, robin, owl, butterfly, etc. Suggest that he move and vocalize like the character he is imitating, and that he assume the posture and facial expression he believes they employ.
   b. Ask the child to imitate the sound of a mosquito, fly, bee, the wind, thunder, an airplane, or a car stuck in the snow.
   c. Suggest that he pretend he's a snowman on a hot day; a dancer on the stage; a ball player (batter, catcher, pitcher, fielder).

87. *Picture Grab Bag Exercises*

Save human interest pictures of people, animals and birds from magazines and newspapers, and drop them in a manila envelope. Ask the child to "grab" a picture without looking, and to make a story about it. Encourage him by asking questions which stimulate thinking such as, "What do you think is happening? How does the boy (or character who is pictured) feel? What is he thinking or saying? What do you think will happen?"

In the beginning, if the youngster finds it difficult to make up a story, you might start him and suggest that he go on. Later when he has learned to let his imagination roam you could take turns at "grabbing" a picture and telling a complete story.

88. *Mind-Stretching Exercises*

To stimulate thinking and to exercise the imagination, encourage the child to express his thoughts on the following subjects. Do not interrupt him, no matter how far out or improbable his ideas seem to you. Ask:

a. How many uses can you think of for a brick? (An unusually creative child may think of 25 or 30.)

How many uses can you think of for a wooden board?
How many ways, besides for writing, could you use a pencil?
How many uses could you find for an empty shoe box? A button? A block? A tissue?

Your youngster may come up with some ideas he would like to try. Excellent!

b. Give the child the opportunity to think how he would handle a difficult situation.

1) What would you do if you were lost in a crowd of people? (This is an opportunity to teach address, father's name, and telephone number.)
2) How could we help a friend, who is inconsiderate, to be more kind and polite?
3) What would you do if you were the Sunday School (or nursery school) teacher?

89. *Make A Story*

This activity stimulates the child's imagination and gives practice in communication. Cut pictures from newspapers, magazines or catalogs, or use cartoon strips that do not have words. Ask the child to make a story and to arrange the pictures in the sequence which corresponds to his story. You may need to do a few stories from pictures with him until he grasps the idea.

90. *Tell A Tale*
The object of this activity is to encourage the imagination. You may start an imaginary story, after a few sentences, stop, and ask the child to continue. Soon he stops, and you go on. Follow this pattern to a reasonable ending.
Suggestions:
Try to use quiet words, funny words, noisy words, scary words, action words. The child will follow your lead.
Example:
Tim and Greg parked their bikes under the drooping willow beside the rushing river. "They're hidden real good," Greg said, looking back, as the boys headed for the river. "I don't see why our mothers don't want us to play near the dam."
"Nobody will know we're here 'cause our bikes can't be seen from the road. Let's go a ways up the river."
The boys went around the curving river bank toward the dam.
(The child continues the story.)

Science

Children have a natural curiosity about nature. We can use this innate trait to foster learning. Soon the child comes to recognize the fact that science answers questions and solves daily problems. If encouraged, he views science as a thrilling study, the door to the unknown.

91. *Make Science Fun*
Suggestions for activities the child will enjoy:
a. Collecting and comparing various types of leaves and learning the identity of the trees and plants from which they came. Teach only the more common trees in your area, beginning with those in your yard and on your street. Talk about the difference between evergreen and deciduous trees. Identify common shrubs which the child sees about him.
b. Learn the names of flowers in your yard and talk about the requirements for plant growth. (Soil, moisture, warmth and light.)
c. Watch for signs of spring—green shoots appearing, buds bursting on the trees, longer days, etc.
d. Walk in the rain, or in the fog. Listen to the rain on the roof. Watch an electrical storm. Walk in the snow.
e. Study cloud formations and look for imaginary figures.

Observe changes in the appearance of the sky at sunrise, sunset, before and during a storm.

f. Notice the difference in coloring of various kinds of birds. Teach the child to identify the more common ones.

g. Watch the night sky. Talk about stars and the moon, and the reason we don't see them on a cloudy night.

h. Watch insects. Learn about the life cycle of insects of special interest.

i. Listen to the wind as it howls down the chimney or whispers through the trees; feel it as it pushes against you while walking.

j. Grow plants from seed and watch the developmental cycle from seed to mature plant to seed.

k. Study plant, animal and insect life through a magnifying glass.

l. Discuss heat and cold. Heat causes water to boil and results in steam. Cold, at a certain degree, causes freezing and results in ice.

92. *The Time Concept*

Preschoolers can absorb the time concept when given direction. Use snapshots and movies of the child's early life. Talk with him about activities he was able to accomplish during his first years. ("You were just learning to crawl in this picture and here you could stand alone. See, in this picture you're reaching for your first birthday cake—you were just one year old.") Go on to milestones in the second year of life through pictures and memoirs.

Make reference to important milestones in his physical development—walking, talking, feeding himself and toilet training. Talk of interesting happenings, "when you were two," (or three or four) and of trips and pleasant experiences.

Point out pictures of your own and of your husband's childhood and tell about events that occurred when you were children.

93. *What Is It Made Of?*

To help the child become aware of the origin of various common objects, place an assortment of things made from glass, wood, plastic, or metal on the table. Talk about them, what they're made of and how they were made. You might, for example, use a water glass, a plastic glass, a tin can and a wooden pencil. Ask the child to find other objects in his home which are made from the various materials.

94. *Birds In Winter*

As motivation to learn about winter birds and also to teach kindness, a child learns much from observing birds at a feeding shelf outside a window. Explain that in winter, when seeds are snow- and ice-covered, the birds welcome food given to them by their human friends. Bread crumbs, seeds, suet and nuts attract various kinds of birds including downy woodpeckers, nuthatches, chickadees, cardinals and bluejays.

The child will note the beauty of the cardinal, the ability of the nuthatch to walk down a tree trunk head first, and the saucy bad manners of the bluejay. He will observe that as the weather grows disagreeable more birds find their way to the feeding shelf. His interest can readily grow to concern for protection of our birds, and with your guidance, can include other forms of wild life.

95. *Animals In Winter*

Talk with your youngster about animals that go into hiding in winter. Some seek shelter and store either food or body fat to live through the cold weather. Some hibernate in dens or caves. Others sleep only when the cold is extreme but move about on warm days.

Animals your child may wish to learn about include woodchucks, bears, raccoons, chipmunks, turtles and snakes.

96. *Shadows*

Demonstrate to your child the fact that shadows are caused by opaque objects with a light at one side. He will learn that shadows are caused by artificial as well as natural light. Have him look for shadows; shadows of clouds on fields and water, shadows (shade) of trees and buildings, and shadows of people in early morning and late afternoon.

As he matures he'll learn that eclipses of the sun and moon are caused by shadows, and that an eclipse may be partial or total. See if he can figure out the reason. (Another opportunity to "look it up.")

Suggestions:
a. Read Robert Louis Stevenson's, *My Shadow.*
b. Observe various sun-originated shadows. Point out the moving shadow as a cloud races across the sun.
c. Make shadows with a flashlight or electric bulb. Try to form shadow animals and birds by manipulating the hands.
d. View an eclipse. Emphasize the danger to the eyes of looking directly at the sun. Probably the best and most safe method is to view the eclipse on TV whenever possible.
e. Draw and color shadow pictures.

97. *The Wind*
Walk with your young child in the wind. Ask, "Can you see the wind?" The child will decide that though he can't see it, he can see the things it does. As you walk, see how many evidences of the wind he can discover. He may say, "It is pushing me. That man has to hold his hat. It is blowing the clothes on the line. It's making the trees bend. It's making the flag snap and the edge is tearing. That boy can hardly make his bike go against it."
Suggestions:
a. Blow up a balloon. Discuss why the balloon gets larger. Watch as father puts air into a tire. Compare the two activities.
b. Blow soap bubbles. How is a soap bubble like a balloon and a tire? Why does the soap bubble break more quickly than the balloon? The balloon more quickly than the tire? Could the tire be broken if enough air was forced into it?

98. *Insects*
Children are interested in insects. Capitalize on this interest as you and your child talk about the benefits and damage brought about by insects. Teach him to observe them. How many legs do they have? How many parts to their body? What do various species eat? Where do they live? Of what use are their feelers?

Other facts the child will be interested in learning are that insects have from two to five eyes which cannot close, that they have outside shells instead of skin, that most fly, though some jump, and that there are more insects in the world than all the other animals put together.

Learn about the life cycle of insects. (Egg, larva, pupa and adult) concentrating on one or two species in which the child is particularly interested. (Most children enjoy the study of butterflies.) Find pictures illustrating the stages in the life of an insect. This is an opportunity for the child to do "research" at the library with your help.

Talk about bees, flies, ants, wasps, moths, butterflies, mosquitoes, crickets, grasshoppers, fleas, lice, termites, and any other insect which interests the youngster. As you discuss methods of controlling insects (birds, insecticides) you'll have the opportunity to get into the subject of ecology. Talk about how insecticides may result in the death of birds because the birds eat poisoned insects. Discuss reasons for mothproofing clothes closets. Think of insects that are our friends. (Butterflies and bees pollinate blossoms, and bees make honey.) Now think of some that are enemies. (Termites, flies, mosquitoes.)

In the autumn or early spring, watch for cocoons. If your child can be fortunate enough to see a moth or butterfly emerge from the cocoon, he'll be thrilled.

After you've studied insects for a time, list the harmful and helpful results of insect life. Try to have the child think of facts to include while you write them as:

Helpful Insects—Bees make honey. Bees and butterflies pollinate flowers. Ants loosen the soil.

Harmful Insects—Flies, fleas, lice and mosquitoes carry disease. Some insects destroy plants. Ants are pests when they get into the house. Moths eat woolen clothing.

99. Make a "Bug House"

Your child can easily make a "bug house" so that he can study the specimens he catches. Cut the top off a milk carton and make windows in the four sides. Place grass and twigs in the bottom and stretch a sheer discarded stocking over the top of the carton. Fasten it with a rubber band. Glue cellophane over the windows.

The youngster will enjoy collecting insects and observing them through the windows. Have him imitate the sounds they make. (Buzzing, whirring, zooming, chirping.)

Make a list of the insects he has collected. Perhaps you can help him identify unfamiliar ones. Talk about creatures that combat insects. (Frogs, lizards, rodents, birds.) This discussion may lead to an interest in the study of frogs, toads, lizards, snakes, mice or birds.

100. Where Does It Come From? (1)

As you and your child live, play and work together, you'll find numerous ways to stimulate his curiosity and to encourage the "let's find out" idea which results in his increased knowledge about life and the world in general. Take time to answer his questions or to help him search out information from the dictionary or encyclopedia.

Interesting topics which he'd like to know about might be the origins of flour, cocoa, sugar, plastic and steel. You and he will find many others that lend themselves to the question, "Where does it come from?"

Adjust the information to your child's interest and maturity. Feed him information only so long as he has an appetite for more.

101. Experiments

Children learn from experiments. Your child may wish to do favorite experiments several times. Encourage him to try experiments and to think why certain results occur. Be sure to stress causes

and effects—the "why" of experiments. Give helpful hints if he is unable to draw accurate conclusions.
Suggestions:
a. Experiment with the causes and effects of freezing and thawing by putting water in the freezer. Later, place the ice in the refrigerator for a few hours. What happens? Why? Remove ice from the freezer and leave it at room temperature. What happens? Put ice outside in the sun on a hot day. What happens?
b. Experiment with air. Place a dry tissue in the bottom of a water glass. Turn the glass upside down and submerge it under water, straight down. The child will be amazed to see the tissue is dry when the glass is removed. See if he can figure out that water was unable to enter the glass when it was filled with air. You can prove to him there is air in the glass by tipping it on the side while it is under water for he'll see bubbles rise to the surface.

Another interesting experiment with air is to punch only one hole in a can of condensed milk and observe that the milk runs very slowly. Punch a second hole in the top of the can and demonstrate how rapidly the milk runs then. You may need to explain that when air rushes into the can through one hole it forces the milk out of the other one.

c. Do experiments with evaporation. On a hot, low humidity day, saturate a cloth with water and hang it outside. See if the child can tell where the water goes.

Repeat the experiment on a cloudy day when the humidity is high. Why does the cloth dry so slowly? (Evaporation does not readily occur when humidity is high.)

Another experiment involving evaporation which is easily demonstrated is the principle observed when food on the range boils dry. Talk with the child about what occurs and where the moisture goes when it leaves the pan, as well as when clothing dries. Such a discussion easily leads into the causes of rain.

You can point out the results of warm moist air coming into contact with a cooler object which results in condensation. This is easily observed by allowing a pitcher of ice water to remain at room temperature for a few minutes. The child will wonder how the moisture got on the outside of the pitcher, and you have an excellent opportunity to explain.

The above experiments are only a sampling of the ones you can do with your child to teach him to question and to seek answers about the world around him. You and he will find mnay others which stimulate him to seek the "why" of science facts. He may like to experiment with growing plants, with properly caring for a pet or with studying objects and living things through a microscope. He may want to know what causes dew, why it snows instead of rains, and vice versa. And when he goes to the doctor for a check-up, ask the medical person to allow the child to listen to his own heartbeat and chest sounds with the stethescope. Opportunities for the child's learning are endless if you but take advantage of them as they present themselves.

The area of science is thoroughly covered by hundreds of children's books. Finding the solution to a question becomes an exciting experience for the child when together you look something up.

102. *The Sun's Heat*

On a hot day place equal amounts of water in two identical dishes. Put one dish outside in direct sunlight, and leave the other inside the house. In about an hour have the child check the temperature of the water in both dishes with his finger.

Ask him why the water in the sun becomes hot while that inside remains cool. Help him discover that the sun's heat warmed the dish that was outside, while the shade of the house kept the water cool in the second dish.

See if the child can draw accurate conclusions as to why we sit under an umbrella or tree on a hot day.

103. *Outer Space*

In this day of space exploration all children are aware of outer space. You can help your child to clarify his concepts by using a model of the solar system and showing him how it functions. With the aid of an elementary science book you can easily make a model of a solar system. Still more simple, though less effective, is to use an overhead electric light to represent the sun while a ball representing the earth is carried about the sun in its orbit. On paper draw the sun with the planets, Mercury, Venus, Earth, Mars, Jupiter, Saturn, Uranius, Neptune and Pluto, each in their orbit, circling the sun. Talk of Earth's closest planet neighbors. Talk about the moon, about how it orbits the earth, about its lack of air, and other facts which the child wonders about.

Discuss gravity, and the lack of it in space. Watch a blast off from Cape Kennedy and a moon landing. You'll be amazed at the amount of understanding your child has for these matters when you gain his interest.

For more information utilize the library. There are many space books which will delight your child.

104. *Where Does It Come From? (2)*

A simple game which helps the child acquire knowledge and which also stimulates the memory may be played as you go about routine household tasks. Ask the child where various common products come from.

Examples:
Wood, glass, paper, woolen clothing, milk, potatoes, bread, oranges, etc.

If the child answers "From the store," ask where the store got it. Trace the origin of the article back to the source, often via factory to farm or forest.

Encourage the child to furnish answers as long as he's able; when he reaches the limit of his information, you should supply answers. After a few days repeat, "Where does it come from?" to see how well he remembers.

105. *Animal, Bird Or Plant*

This game teaches the child to classify and to think rapidly. Print the words, animal, plant and bird on three pieces of cardboard. Tell the child you will say the name of one of the classifications and he is to hold up the correct identifying card before you count to ten. (If you said, "Owl," he'd hold up the bird card.) Continue as long as the child is interested.

Suggestions for playing the game might include:
Dog, oak tree, blue jay, lion, cat, lettuce, chickadee, squirrel, camel, rose, sparrow, pine tree, parakeet, penguin, whale, zebra, grass, wren.

Variations:

Make cards for the following classifications, and play the game in the same way.

a. Animals, trees, flowers. (Maple, chrysanthemum, deer, etc.)
b. Trees, fruits, vegetables. (Elm, oranges, carrots, etc.)
c. Birds, fish, animals. (Cardinal, trout, moose, etc.)
d. Reptiles, mammals, rocks. (Alligator, kitten, granite, etc.)

106. *Collections*

Children love to make collections. Capitalize on this inclination to encourage learning in the science area. Support the child by showing interest in his collections of rocks, leaves, flowers, shells, seeds and other science related areas no matter how strange they may seem to you. Discuss his collections with him and when he reveals interest, assist him in locating books so that he can delve more deeply into the subject.

Show the child how to preserve his collections.
Examples:
a. Glue small rocks on cardboard. Print identifying names below the specimens.
b. Leaves, properly identified, may be pressed until dry and mounted on construction paper. Fresh leaves may be preserved by placing them between two sheets of wax paper and pressing them with a warm iron. Have your youngster make sets of gift place mats by this method.
c. Seeds may be preserved in small cellophane bags and glued to cardboard. Identify each specimen.
d. Flowers may be pressed until dry, then mounted and identified.
e. Picture collections of birds and wild and domestic animals make interesting collections when made into bird and animal books. If he has the maturity, the child may wish to write a story below each picture.

107. *Magnets*
Magnets fascinate children. Use this interest to help the child learn about magnetism. If he has a toy magnet he will make these discoveries:
a. He can pick up a number of tacks, pins or nails, each supported by the one above it.
b. Hard steel objects will become temporarily magnetized by stroking them with a bar magnet.
c. Like poles of two magnets repel one another and unlike ones attract.
d. The child will become interested in the compass and can gain some understanding of how it operates. This can lead to discussion of the importance of the compass to navigators and explorers.
e. Magnets will likely lead to a discussion of electricity. If you do not feel equal to an explanation, use the opportunity to look the subject up in a children's encyclopedia. Be frank in admitting you sometimes need to look up information, and that you enjoy learning with your child.
Some experiments your child might try:
a. Lay a nail on top of the table and move the nail by sliding the magnet along the under side of the table directly below the nail.
b. Drop a nail in a glass. By lifting the magnet along the side of the glass, the nail will climb out as it follows the magnet.

108. *The Seasons*
 Suggestions:
 a. Talk with the child about the seasons, summer, winter, spring and fall. Discuss causes for the changes of season. (If you need to refresh your memory look up "Season" in the encyclopedia.) Talk about the changes in weather and the effects upon humans, animals and plants.
 b. The youngster might enjoy cutting seasonable pictures from magazines which illustrate the four seasons, then classifying and pasting them in a scrapbook.
 c. Print *Yes* and *No* on two cards. As you make statements about the seasons the child holds up the *Yes* card if they are correct, the *No* card if incorrect.
 Suggestions for statements:
 a. There is snow in summer.
 b. Leaves fall from the trees in the spring.
 c. Christmas comes in the winter.
 d. New Year's Day comes in the spring.
 e. Children have vacation from school in the summer.
 f. Many birds fly south in the fall.
 g. Bears sleep all summer.
 h. Birds make nests in the spring.
 i. People rake leaves in the fall.
 j. We swim at the lake in the summer.
 k. Valentine's Day is in the summer.
 l. People make gardens in the spring.
 m. Easter comes in the summer.
 n. Halloween comes in the fall.
 o. Apples are picked in the spring.

109. *Fact Or Fantasy*
 Help your child separate fact from fantasy by discussing myths about insects. Some common superstitions which frequently are quoted are:
 a. It will rain if you step on an ant.
 b. Spider webs in a house are a sign of prosperity.
 c. Killing a spider will bring poverty to the killer.
 d. A spider in a shell hung about the neck is good for the health of the wearer.
 e. A yellow honeybee is a sign of good news, but a black one designates bad news.
 f. Crickets bring good luck.
 g. Dragonflies are capable of "sewing up" parts of the body such

as eyelids, ears, lips or nostrils.

h. A ball of cotton hung on a string in the doorway will prevent flies from entering.

Social Behavior

Children need to be taught the type of social behavior which will help them to live in modern society in such a way that their basic needs are met without depriving others of their rights. (See Chapter Five, pages 21—28.

110. *Teaching Neatness and Order*

The months between 18 and 36 are important ones in the formation of habits of neatness and order. Your time is well spent in providing such training for from it a child gains a sense of independence from adult assistance. If you let him grow past this important sensitive period without helping him to develop habits of independence and orderliness, you may find it difficult to change the pattern in later years.

Suggestions:

a. Low shelves for books and games.

b. A toy box for holding small toys and blocks.

c. A low clothes rod and hooks at his height which encourage the child to hang up clothing.

d. Make neatness a game. Bend a wire clothes hanger into a circle. Staple a plastic bag to the hanger to make a basket. Hang it over a door in the child's room and suggest that he "make a basket" with dirty clothes as he undresses.

c. Attach a shoe bag to the back of the closet door. The various pockets hold caps, mittens, scarves and other small items within the child's reach.

111. *Learning About The Family*
Suggestions:

a. Talk about members of the immediate family. Discuss the relative ages starting with parents and proceeding to the youngest member. To help the child form concepts of time talk about which family members have lived longer.

Suggest that the child draw pictures of the family group.

b. Talk about relationships of grandparents, uncles, aunts and cousins.

c. Look at family pictures. Children enjoy seeing and hearing about their parents' experiences when they were young, and they

also like to know about their own and their siblings' baby days.
d. Keep current snapshots of your family group, including grandparents, uncles, aunts and cousins posted near the telephone. When your preschooler has a phone conversation with a family member, point to the picture so he can see the person with whom he's speaking.

112. *Television*
Parents need to protect children from certain programs glorifying violence lest the media become the prime influence that guides the consciousness of children. You can guide your child to a more optimistic future by shielding him from unnecessary and damaging scenes of violence which can cause confusion and inability to differentiate between meaningless and worthwhile goals. To a child life seems pallid compared to the excitement of violent programs in which serious problems are created and solved in 30 or 60 minutes.

Carefully screen the programs your child views. There are excellent ones, some of which amuse as they teach the child to cope with difficult social situations, and some promote learning in the academic sense.

113. *Role Playing*
The most natural thing for children to do is to act or pretend. They role play for fun when they're alone, and they role play with friends.
Suggestions:
a. Encourage role playing activities by keeping a box filled with old hats, shoes and clothing. Place a wall mirror at the child's eye level. He'll enjoy seeing his image as he changes roles and costumes.
b. Teach the child how to make and respond to introductions. Pretend you're introducing him to an adult; to a new child; to a relative he's never met before.

When he's able to respond properly, reverse roles and have him introduce you to his playmate's mother or father; to a new friend; to his nursery school or public school teacher.
c. Include role playing for any social situation with which your child needs training, such as talking on the telephone, answering the door, or responding properly when spoken to by an adult.

114. *What Did Mother Do?*
Start a story about a hypothetical child who is very oppositional. (Wants something at the store, doesn't want to go to bed, disobeys,

etc.) Break off at the climax where the child is extremely objectionable. Ask, "What did Mother do?"

This method is an effective way of leading into a discussion of a problem area for the youngster is not threatened since you're discussing a hypothetical child.

115. *Did You Do Something Nice Today?*

At bedtime ask the child if he can recall something nice he did for someone during the day. If he is unable to recall anything, with your help he might plan a kind act he could perform the next day.

Another thought-stimulating question you might use is, "Did someone do something nice for you today?"

116. *Being Helpful*

As you and your child think of ways to be kind, polite or helpful, you might list them on a chart in manuscript writing. Keep the words simple and the sentences short so that as the child begins to recognize words he will attempt to read his chart.

Perhaps he'd like to decorate his chart with pictures of people helping one another.

Hang the chart in a prominent place for a few days.

117. *What Do Parents Do?*

Many children do not understand the nature of their parents' work. Explain as clearly as possible and attempt to arrange a visit, if this is permitted. Read stories about the parents' type of work. Stress reasons for working and the contributions made to the community, and society in general, which result from both parents' type of employment.

Your child might enjoy drawing pictures of his father or mother at work, or he might like role playing as he pretends to be one or the other. You can gain an accurate assessment of his understanding of the work his parents do.

118. *What Work Do They Do?*

As you talk about the various types of work people do to earn a living, try to instill in the child's mind an awareness of the dignity of work and a respect for services performed by various types of workers. Depending upon his interest and maturity, you might discuss and observe the following types of workers: Mechanics, truck drivers, carpenters, electricians, construction workers including road, bridge and building construction, telephone repairmen, plumbers, hospital workers, community workers such as firemen, policemen, postmen and milkmen, and office workers. Include professional workers such as teachers, ministers, attorneys, doctors and engineers.

Children also are interested in what people do in factories and in stores. The list of occupations is almost endless, but you'll likely discuss only one or two at a time as the opportunity presents itself.

119. Who Am I?

After discussion of several types of work you can determine the child's understanding by using riddles. Give clues as:

a. I use saws, hammers and nails. I work with wood and other building materials. I sometimes work outdoors, but I also work inside. Who am I? (Carpenter)

b. I work on motors and on other parts of cars, trucks and airplanes. I try to make them run as they should. I get dirty and greasy, but my work is interesting and necessary. Who am I? (Mechanic)

Encourage the child to make riddles about types of work in which he asks you, "Who am I?"

120. Teaching Moral Judgment

You can stimulate the development of the child's moral judgment by raising leading questions about difficult moral dilemmas, and then letting the child have his say. Get his undivided attention, perhaps at dinner or just before sleep in the evening. The best time for a discussion is after he has done something right. Praise him for what he did and ask his reasons. Then listen to him. Usually families that encourage children to express opinions and who listen without necessarily agreeing, produce youngsters with a high level of morality. It seems that when children are exposed to moral reasoning a stage above their own, they usually prefer it.

Suggestions for discussion: (Adjust the problems you pose to the child's level of maturity.) Ask, "What would you do?"

a. If you accidentally knocked a boy down?
b. If a child tripped you each time you walked past him?
c. If you saw two larger boys teasing a smaller child?
d. If you found a quarter in someone's yard?
e. If children were making fun of a crippled child?
f. If you saw an injured kitten lying beside the road?
g. If Mother asked you to come home at 5:30, but at that time you were in the middle of an exciting game at a friend's home?
h. If you broke a dish your friend's mother liked very much, and no one saw you do it?
i. If children laughed at you when you made a mistake?

121. *Consideration For Others*
Dramatize with the child two or three examples of "good" and "bad" behavior toward others.
   Examples:
   a. "Good" behavior. The first person holds the door and waits patiently for the other to pass through.
      One person picks up something that belongs to another and returns it to the owner.
   b. "Bad" behavior. The first person runs through the door allowing it to slam in the other's face.
      One person kicks the possession of another out of the way, or picks it up and puts it into his pocket.

122. *Think Positively*
At a time when you and the child are relaxed, a brief discussion of pleasant, polite or helpful acts performed during the day aids the child in the formation of positive attitudes. Make it a two-way discussion with both of you participating. This is a time when the child may be commended for "nice things you've done today," as well as for both of you to recall considerate, courteous actions of family members and friends.
Do not make this a lecture period!

123. *Fun With The Family*
The following exercise will lead into a discussion of family activities and of the part each member plays in a smooth-running family. It is also a time to talk about family recreation, games and holiday gatherings.
Ask the child to search through old magazines for pictures of families having a good time. After cutting out the pictures he might paste them in a scrapbook. Suggest that he tell a story about the pictures.

124. *Guess Who*
Pretend to be a person who is well-known to the child. Convey clues by expression, gesture and verbal comment. Have him guess who you're imitating.
Encourage him to "act out" another person's personality and appearance as you guess the identity of the character.
This activity gives the opportunity to emphasize desirable and undesirable traits of character without lecturing.

125. *Using The Newspaper*
   Children can grasp the concept that newspapers give current news and they gain an awareness of human emotions before they are able to read. Have the child clip pictures which may be classified under various titles, such as:

         It Makes Us Happy   It Is Funny
         It Makes Us Sad   I Want To Be

   Pictures may be arranged under the proper title in a scrapbook or on a bulletin board. It is best to concentrate on one area for the period of time during which the child shows interest. However, if he discovers additional pictures which may be used in an "old" section, he likely will wish to add them to the proper group.

   As human interest pictures of babies, children, adults, animals and birds portraying amusing, thoughtful or sad feelings are found, you can help the child to become aware of the feelings of others and to develop his skill in observation and imagination if you ask, "What are they saying?" Encourage him to include what the character in the picture is thinking, and what his next actions may be.

126. *Puppets*
   In play with puppets a child will reveal the areas in which he has strong feelings, and you'll get clues to his sense of values. Many children hesitate to express their feelings about home, parents, school and friends. Puppets provide an excellent means for encouraging them to speak, for they find it easy to express ideas and feelings through puppets since it is not they that speak, but the characters represented by the puppets.

   If you have concern about your child's feelings in certain areas, (relationship to brothers, sisters, parents, friends) suggest that he make the puppets talk. Often you'll also discover clues to his feelings about himself. However, regardless of feelings that come out in puppet play, you should not comment on the remarks the puppets make or you may not get an accurate expression of the child's feelings in future play.

   There are fine sets of commercial puppets, a complete family being the most valuable for our purpose; or, you may make a simple set which will serve the purpose. Stick puppets consisting of paper figures pasted on one end of a tongue depressor or cardboard are easily and quickly constructed by you with the child's help.

   A second type of puppets which are easily made are finger puppets. Roll a paper into a cylinder which is large enough to contain the index finger. The head may be cut from a magazine or drawn by you or the child. Paste it on stiff paper so that it will remain erect when attached to the cylinder. Add yarn hair, facial features, hats, etc., as desired. The child may also wish to give his puppets arms, which can be attached to the cylinder.

Hand puppets are another type which can be made from cloth or paper. Use a pattern such as this:

Cut two identical shapes from stiff paper, cloth or felt. Staple or sew them together. Facial features, hair, buttons and belts add to the identity of the puppet character.

The child may operate his puppets from behind the edge of the table if he wishes a stage. He may prefer operating them without a stage by holding them up as they talk.

127. Guessing Game

To help the child realize the extent to which he depends upon vision, blindfold him and ask him to walk until he touches something with his hands. See if he can describe and identify the object without peeping.

Try this experiment in the yard as you lead the child. He will readily appreciate the importance of his eyesight. Talk about the way he felt when he was "blind."

You can stress the importance of hearing by turning the sound down on a TV program which he's watching. See if he can tell what is happening without hearing the accompanying sounds and conversation. Encourage him to express his frustration.

This type of activity paves the way for a discussion of handicapped children, and of the ways in which normal people can help the handicapped.

128. How Would You Feel?

Ask your youngster to pretend he is the child in the following stories, and to tell how he thinks he might have felt.

a. Ronnie saved his money and bought a box of crayons like the ones his neighbor Bill had. When Bill came to play at Ronnie's, he saw the crayons. He shouted that his crayons had been stolen and accused Ronnie of taking them.

How would you have felt if you'd been Ronnie?

b. John's mother was in the hospital and he was living at a neighbor's home. At school he had trouble keeping his mind on his work. He made many mistakes and got a poor grade on his paper.

At recess Jim, who had a perfect paper, called John a "dummy." John put his head down and walked away.

How would you have felt if you'd been John?

129. Finish The Story

Mr. and Mrs. Ellis adopted an eight-year-old girl from Viet Nam. One day they found her crying with her clothing torn. A group of children were staring at her.

Finish the story telling what you think had happened. How did the girl feel? How did the other children feel?

130. Likes And Dislikes

You can guide your child to evaluate his social behavior through discussion. One way to lead into a positive discussion is through a story in which a hypothetical child behaved appropriately in an embarrassing or annoying situation. Ask, "What did you like about the way Tom behaved? Do you think another child might have said rude things?" Try to formulate questions which will bring appropriate responses.

You may proceed to a discussion of your child's behavior by saying something like, "We all have things we like about ourselves. Think a minute, then tell me what you like about yourself." If he is unable to respond, help him by suggesting that you admire his truthfulness, good nature, kindness, helpfulness, or whatever trait you feel applies. By first "accentuating the positive," you have set the stage for moving into the realms of social behavior in which your child needs improvement. You may suggest that everyone has areas in which they would like to improve. Point out your awareness of your own weak areas. (He already knows them but will admire your honesty in admitting to shortcomings.) Play it by ear in the discussion, and when you feel the time is right, ask if there are situations with which he has trouble, or in which he feels uncomfortable. He may say he becomes angry when he can't do something he wishes, when he's teased or corrected, that he's not always truthful, etc.

Ask how he feels after an experience in which he "lost control" of himself. Did he feel happy? Did he like himself? Talk the problem out with the child without criticising or lecturing, but lead him by asking what he thinks he might do "the next time." He may have several suggestions. Guide him toward the most realistic one. And recognize with the child the extreme difficulty of controlling one's self, but stress the fact that each time he deals successfully with a problem, he will feel happier, will grow in strength to meet the problem the next time, and will like himself better.

In conclusion of a discussion topic the child might be led to generalize that inappropriate social behavior results in unhappy experiences and possible loss of the respect of others. Examples of discussion topics:
 a. How to respond to teasing.
 b. How to respond to embarrassment about failure.
 c. How to meet new people.
 d. How to respond to interruption when occupied in an interesting project.
 e. How to handle prejudice toward minority group children.
 f. How to handle one's self after losing one's temper.
 g. What to do when you know you were in the wrong.
 h. How to handle the problem of necessary, but disliked, chores.

Reading And Phonics

There is universal agreement that reading is a highly desirable skill. In the modern world reading is a necessity, and the person who reads poorly is at a great disadvantage. Because parents and teachers are well aware of the importance of reading, in their desire to help children, they sometimes fail because they disregard individual differences. An occasional child may be emotionally, intellectually and physically ready to read at age three, while another may not be sufficiently developed and motivated until age seven or eight. The average child falls somewhere between the two extremes.

There is much that you can do to lay a proper foundation for your child's success in reading. The youngster's response to your attempts to create a desire for reading is your clue as to whether or not you are proceeding at the proper rate for success. So long as he is interested, you are on safe ground, but when he is bored, frustrated or reluctant to continue an activity, the project should be discontinued. Adult pressure for success in reading before children are sufficiently mature to meet with success often results in severe reading problems in later years.

Your child will meet with his level of success and will find joy in reading experiences if you hold tenaciously to one idea—keep it fun!
(Reread Chapter Six, pages 39-42.

131. *Stimulate Interest In Reading*
Read, read, read to your child. Read to increase his knowledge, listening ability and for enjoyment. Remember that his level of comprehension is much higher than his vocabulary. Perhaps the story or pictures remind him of something he wishes to tell you. Encourage

him to interrupt you to talk about whatever he likes.

At any time of day or night reading is a good way to soothe a weary or frightened child, or to entertain a restless one. Hold him on your lap or sit close to him so that you're brought close together by touch as well as talk.

Suggestions:
a. Keep reading a pleasure, never a task. The child should regard a story as an interesting shared experience.
b. Your attitude toward adult reading influences your child's feelings and interest in the activity.
c. Regular trips to the library should be established by age three.
d. At age three a child's interest may be stimulated by reading highway and advertising signs, labels, and directions that come with games. He will readily learn the signs, "Mens' Room" and "Ladies' Room"—in fact anything that helps him to understand that printed letters form words which tell us something.
e. Your child's interests will be your best guide as to the type of books you'll read to him. He may prefer factual books that explain the world rather than fantasy. Try to guide him to choose books which challenge his thinking. If a book is of the proper level of difficulty, he'll likely ask you to read it over and over. If it's too easy, or too difficult, he'll be restless.

Two- and three-year-olds often enjoy simple factual stories about small children, animals, what grown-ups do, and the world outside the home. In poetry they like nursery rhymes, modern children's poems, nonsense rhymes and rhymes that have meaning.
f. Encourage the child to memorize favorite short rhymes and poems. As you read poems that have repetitive parts, he will like to repeat them with you. Soon he will have memorized the jingle or rhyme.
g. Allow the youngster to choose books to own on special occasions, and provide him with a place to keep them—his own shelf or bookcase can be a prized possession.

132. *Interest In Letter Forms*

Your child is beginning to grasp the idea that reading is another kind of language, that it is talk written down. Point out the titles on books, labels on boxes, and the names on records. Show him what his name looks like. If he's interested in printing his name, teach him. (See Exercise 133.)

You may write notes to him and pin them in conspicuous places. When he asks what the words say, tell him. If he shows eagerness to learn more, use the following exercises in this section to teach him. You can determine by his attitude whether he's ready to learn letter names.

133. *Teaching The Alphabet, Numerals or Child's Name*

Make large letters, numerals or the child's name on cardboard with a crayon or magic marker. The child will use the printing as a model, so make it accurate. (See Exercise 53.)

As a warm-up activity, have him "write in the air" the letters he will make. (Exercise 47.)

Place an inch layer of sand on dark construction paper in the bottom of a large shallow box. Encourage the child to write in the sand the symbols you wish to teach. Later, when you're sure he can be successful, suggest that he make letters, numerals or his name on the blackboard or on a large sheet of unlined paper.

134. *Teaching The Alphabet* (Continued)

This exercise is a guide for teaching the alphabet. It gives the order in which letters may be taught. You'll refer to it often, but will use various other techniques to stimulate learning as explained in the following exercises. Remember to select an activity which you feel is appropriate for your child's level of maturity.

Suggestions:

a. Play a game to teach the child "what the letters say." Suppose you were going to teach the letter *M*. You might repeat a sentence containing several *M* words as, "Mary asked her mother for a mug of milk."

Suggest that the child listen for the *M* sounds as you repeat the sentence. Make the sound for him and ask him to repeat it, as *m-m-m mother, m-m-m Mary,* etc. Tell him the *M* sound is the one we make when something tastes good. If he's still interested, you may think together of more *M* words as you write them in manuscript printing. Ask the child to draw a circle around each *M* as he sees you write it, and to make the *M* sound each time.

As he learns a letter, encourage him to look for it on signs, packages, in magazines, newspapers and on TV. Remember to keep the activity light, happy and relaxed. At first he may forget the sounds of letters. Tell him at once what the sound is without criticism or making him struggle or guess. Praise him when he knows a sound, or thinks of a word to correspond to a sound you're teaching.

Keep letter teaching sessions short, three to five minutes at a time, but if the child enjoys it the activity may be done several times a day. If he's uninterested, discontinue the work for a few weeks, then cautiously try again.

b. Other letters you'll teach, and some helpful associations follow:

h looks something like a chair *w* the windy sound (w-w-w-w)
p the puffing sound (p-p-p-p) *r* a growling dog (r-r-r-r)
s a hissing snake (s-s-s-s) *t* a ticking clock (t-t-t-t)

c. By the time your child has mastered the above consonant sounds, which always are consistent, he is ready for the first vowel. The vowels, a, e, i, o and u, each have more than one sound, and every word must contain at least one vowel. When teaching the first vowel you might start with the short sound of a, as in apple. When the child has mastered this sound he is ready to combine it with some of the consonants he has learned. Together you can sound it out and write such words as hat, rat, mat, pat, and sat, for he already knows these sounds. Soon he will recognize familiar sounds in the middle and end of words as well as at the beginning.

Don't insist that the child sound out words he knows. Use this technique as a key he may use to unlock new combinations of sounds which make up words.

d. Teach the remaining letters in this approximate order: j, l, z, b, d, short e, then k and g as in goat, c as in cat, f, short i, then n, short o, u and y followed by q, v, and x.

Next you're ready to teach the long sounds of the vowels. Tell the child that vowels with the long sound say their own name. *Examples:*

Long a—ate, plane; long e—easy, meat; long i—ice, Ida; long o—open, more; long u—use, beautiful.

Examples of the short vowel sounds:

Short a—apple, fat; short e—fed, end; short i—in, it; short o—on, not; short u—us, bus.

135. *Frame A Letter*

An effective way to introduce new letters is to print one letter per 8½ x 11 inch page with a magic marker, thus:

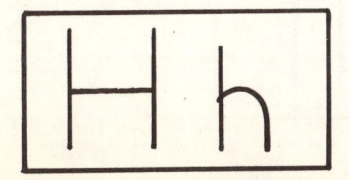

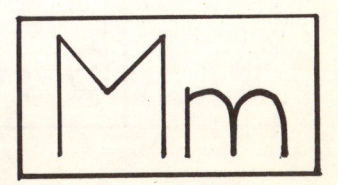

On the reverse side of the page place a picture and word which starts with the letter, as, house and man.

Make a construction paper frame to fit over the pages approximately 8 x 10 inches in size. Frame the letter you are teaching and hang it at the child's eye level. Talk about the letter and name the sound it makes in words. Think of words starting with that sound. See if the child can think of others.

Teach only one letter at a time, often reviewing the ones previously taught. Don't hurry! Your child will only become confused and discouraged if you present new material before he has thoroughly mastered the old.

136. *Letter Puzzles*
An activity which will reinforce letter names and sounds as it provides practice in visual discrimination and coordination is the solving of easily made letter puzzles. On cardboard, paste a picture and print the letter with which it begins as:

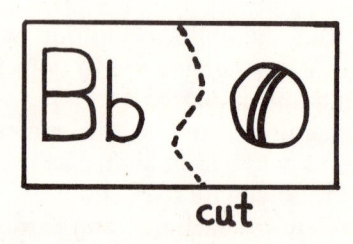

[Bb | ball picture]
cut

Cut between the letter and picture in such a way that the letter will not match any other card. "Scramble" several puzzle cards using the letters and sounds which have been taught.

137. *Learning About Letters*
a. When your child is able to match sounds with pictures as in Exercise 136, turn the puzzle card over and replace the picture with the remainder of the word as:

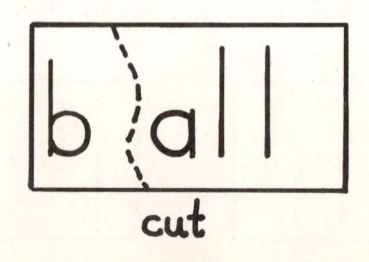

[b | all]
cut

b. When the child is learning to identify letters, give him exercises such as the following. Ask him to put an "x" on boxes that are the same:

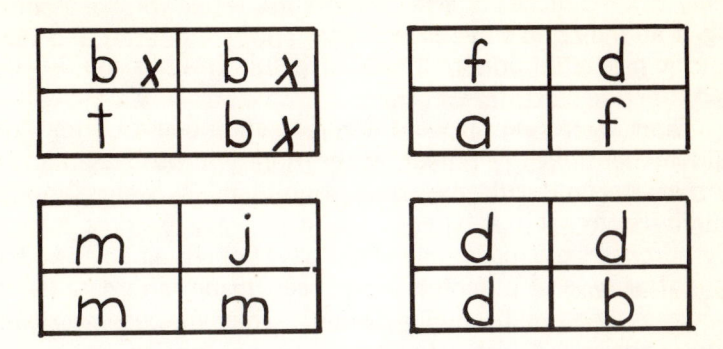

b x	b x
t	b x

f	d
a	f

m	j
m	m

d	d
d	b

c. Make a set of alphabet cards. Ask the child to choose a card, to name it, and to tell the next three letters that follow it in the alphabet. Repeat as long as the child is interested.

d. For more practice in alphabetical order, make a set of alphabet cards including both capital and small letters. On the front put the letter and word, as: *A a apple;* on the back of the card draw or paste a picture of an apple. Continue through the alphabet as:

A a apple	J j jump rope	S s soap
B b bear	K k kite	T t towel
C c coat	L l lamp	U u uniform
D d dog	M m man	V v vase
E e egg	N n nose	W w wall
F f farm	O o orange	X x xylophone
G g ghost	P p pencil	Y y yarn
H h house	Q q quail	Z z zebra
I i ice cream	R r rose	

e. When he shows the proper readiness have your child compile a book of sounds which contains a page for each letter of the alphabet. Use copies of old magazines and suggest that he cut out pictures of objects which begin with the sounds of the various letters and paste them on the proper pages.

138. *At The Supermarket*

To provide practice in recognition of sounds, you might say, "There are hundreds of items at the supermarket. Can you think of something that starts with the same sound as "muffin?" The child might say, "Meat."

Other suggestions:
soup (soap)	duck (dates)	pie (potatoes)
juice (jello)	butter (buns)	fruit (friedcakes)

139. *Shopping*
To give additional practice in beginning sounds, use the following exercise:

Start by saying, "I went shopping and bought butter." Ask the child to continue by repeating the item you purchased and to add another starting with the same sound, as, "I went shopping and bought butter and a bike." The game may become humorous if silly purchases are made. (He might have bought a baby or a baboon.)

After several purchases have been made, alternate leaders and change to another beginning sound. Then he becomes leader and chooses the sound with which he starts.

140. *Reading Signs*
On cardboard print common signs which a child needs to know when outside the home. Tell him that if he knows these signs it is easier to get along in public places. Let him demonstrate his knowledge when away from home. Some signs he should recognize are: Stop, Danger, Exit, Mens', Ladies', Keep Out and Keep Off The Grass.

141. *Encouraging Reading And Number Skills*
Use large easy to handle seeds such as corn, sunflower seeds or beans. You might also use shell macaroni, or small rocks instead of seeds for this project. Ask the child to:
a. Make the alphabet by drawing a letter with Elmer's Glue on construction paper and quickly placing seeds, macaroni or rocks on the moist glue.
b. Make words or sentences.
c. Make numerals.
d. Make addition and subtraction combinations, including the sums and differences.

142. *Giants*
If there are specific sounds with which your child has difficulty this exercise will give him additional practice. Make large capital letters 12 inches high from construction paper. With a ruler draw lines one inch wide across the letter. Ask the child to help you think of words which start with the designated sound. Put them on the lines. Ask him to read them back to you. Save the giant letters for review at another time.

ball
bat
boy
bike

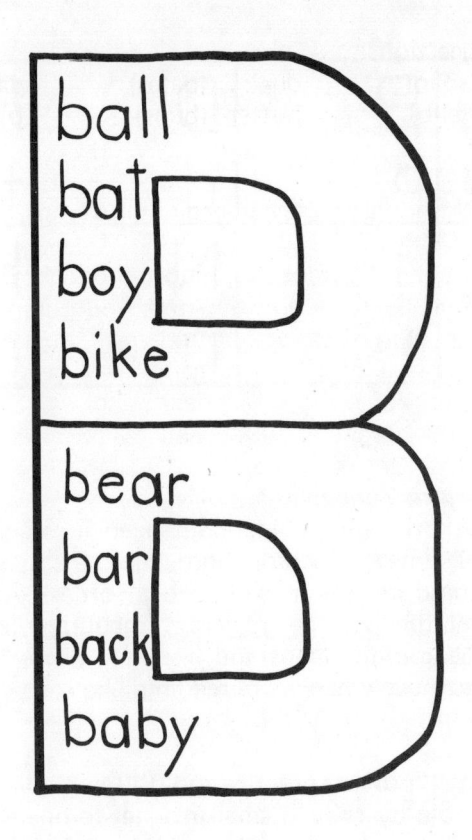

bear
bar
back
baby

143. *Tape Recorded Stories*
When you are especially busy the tape recorder can teach as it entertains your youngster.
   a. When you have available time dictate some of your child's favorite stories. He'll enjoy following the story in the book as the tape plays, and he'll learn to read as he listens and follows. The possibilities for this type of learning are almost limitless so long as you choose stories for taping that he especially likes.
   b. Encourage the child to make original stories while you print them in his words. Tape his stories and suggest that he follow the printed words of "his" story as he listens.

144. *Draw Pictures To Fit The Sounds*
To help the child associate sounds with objects, divide a piece of paper into four, six or eight sections. Put a letter in each division. Ask the child to draw a picture in the proper section which starts with that sound. (B b ball, T t tie, etc.)

R r	P p	D d	F f
L l	T t	N n	H h

145. *How Sharp Are Your Eyes?*

To provide drill and to increase speed in scanning, print the alphabet several times. Include both capital and small letters so arranged that they are not in alphabetical order. Ask the child to quickly circle all the b's, the g's, etc. Encourage left to right eye movement as he rapidly scans the lines of letters "because that's the way our eyes move when we're reading."

146. *Fishing*

This game will provide practice and drill in reading and numbers. Make a fishing pole by tying a small magnet to one end of a 15 inch string which is fastened to the stick. Select a few letters on which the child needs practice, together with many old, easy ones, and print them on 3 x 5 inch cards. Put a paper clip on the corner of each card and place them face down in a shallow dish which represents the lake.

The child fishes by picking up the cards as the magnet touches the paper clip. If he recognizes the letter he catches, he may keep it. If he doesn't know it, tell him, after which he throws it back. Continue until all the fish are caught. If he becomes tired or restless perhaps you haven't included enough easy material. "Fishing" can be discouraging unless one has considerable success.

Variations:

a. Younger children will enjoy fishing for colors. Place several cards of the colors you wish to teach in the lake. Have the child catch, name and match the colors until all the "fish" are in the proper piles. (See Exercises 25 and 26.)

b. Fish for words. Use many old words and some on which he needs additional practice.

c. Fish for numerals and capital and small letters. Place the numerals in one pile and match the capital and small letters. (A a, B b, C c, etc.)

d. Place addition and subtraction combinations in the lake, with answers on separate cards. As the child catches a card, he lays it aside and fishes for the correct answer. When he finds an answer he places it with the combination to which it belongs. (If he has caught 4 + 2, he'll lay it aside until he catches 6.)

147. *Letter Bingo*
Prepare a card with letters in the squares rather than numerals as in regular Bingo. As you call out letters the child marks them with chocolate bits or raisins. When he has completed a row up or across, he calls, "Bingo!" He may then eat the markers.

```
C L T U T Y G X
A N T S R Q M W
C B O V U L X Y
D E C I K Z A B
H G F O I J K R
Q I U P V F X A
```

148. *Shortcuts To Reading*
Some groups of words almost always sound the same. We refer to words which contain the same group of letters, and which rhyme, as a word "family." The most common families are words ending with all, at, ank, aw, er, ink, ight, or, and oy.

By teaching the child to combine these parts of words with beginning consonant sounds, he will increase his reading vocabulary more rapidly.

Example:
Ball, call, fall, hall, mall, stall, tall, wall.
Cat, fat, hat, mat, pat, rat, sat.

149. *Consonant Sounds*
To give the child practice in hearing and recognizing the sounds of beginning consonants have him cut out pictures of objects, people and animals and mount them on cardboard, construction paper or filing cards.

When he has a number of mounted pictures, have him sort them according to the sounds of the beginning consonants (b, d, m, etc.) placing each one in an envelope labeled with the correct letter. (Pictures of a boy, barn, baby, bike, and bee would be placed in the B envelope.)

Occasionally the child will like to mix all of the cards and see how quickly he can resort them again returning them to the correct envelope.

Variation:

When he has thoroughly mastered the beginning single consonant sounds the child could profit from the same type of activity by using consonant blends, (words that begin with bl, cl, fl, gl, pl, sl, spl, squ, br, cr, fr, gr, pr, dr, spr, str, sm, sn, sp, sw, st, sk, scr, thr, tr, tw, th, ch, wh, ph, sh, shr).

Use only a few consonant blends at a time and use the more common blends in the first few exercises of this kind. (Th, sh, st, br, pl, ch, wh.)

Example:

Black, blow, blue, blade.
Clean, clam, clear, cluck.

150. *Climbing The Hill*

This exercise is designed to give practice in beginning sounds combined with familiar endings. Draw a hill on the chalkboard or on paper. Write words at intervals going up the hill. The child climbs by saying the printed word, then thinks of another that begins with the same sound. When he reaches the top, he turns and tries to see how fast he can run down, "without falling," by again giving the words together with the ones he thought of with the same beginning sounds.

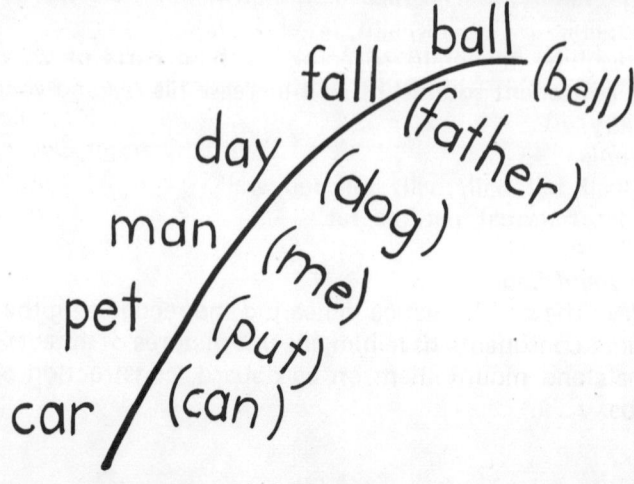

ball (bell)
fall (father)
day (dog)
man (me)
pet (put)
car (can)

151. *Word Recognition*
When the child is interested in looking for familiar words in printed material, this exercise will give him speed in scanning the page for information.
Using any easy, favorite book, ask him to see how quickly he can locate specific words which you select from the page. Choose words which he recognizes such as look, run, come, and see. To make the game more exciting, time him with the second hand on the clock.

152. *Alphabetical Order Activities*
a. You may start the game by thinking of a word that starts with *a* as "ant." The child continues as he thinks of a word which begins with a *b* as "boy." Continue, alternating turns throughout the alphabet. If the child is unable to think of a word you may give him a clue or a helpful hint.
b. As you and the child think of words for each letter of the alphabet, print them in alphabetical order. Ask him to read as many as he can recall. Give clues or tell him when he has trouble.
c. Make a list of short easy words and print them on 3 x 5 cards. Have the child arrange them in alphabetical order, then read the completed list.

153. *Make A Movie*
For additional work on the alphabet and on the sounds of the letters, have the child find pictures that illustrate beginning sounds of the letters A through Z. Paste the pictures on 9 x 12 sheets of paper with the identifying letter in the corner. Attach the papers together in a strip by pasting or using tape.
Take a strong shoe box and two rollers from paper towels. Fasten one end of the strip to each roller. Cut a rectangular opening in the bottom of the box large enough so the pictures may be viewed through it. Insert the roll into the box and check the location where ends of the roll should protrude from the box. Cut holes large enough to accommodate the rollers. Turn the roller and view the pictures like a filmstrip. You and the child will think of many ways to use this idea. Save the rollers and the child will soon have a collection of "films."

154. *Missing Letters*
To provide drill in alphabetical order, prepare these exercises and ask the child to put in the missing letters.
    a. a b c d _ f g _ _ j k l m _ _ _ q r _ t u _ w _ y z

   b. A _ C _ _ F G H _ _ _ L M _ O P Q _ _ _ _ V W _ _ Z
  c. What comes after?
     a _ _   j _ _   l _ _   x _ _   i _ _
     m _ _   v _ _   c _ _   p _ _   r _ _
  d. What comes between?
     a _ c   e _ g   j _ l   h _ j   m _ o
     g _ i   k _ m   u _ w   x _ z   b _ d
     b _ d   n _ p   f _ h   q _ s   p _ r

155. *Match Them*

Use the chalkboard or make a "master list" of words which your child recognizes. Make matching word cards and place them face down on the table.

The child selects a card, pronounces it and finds the corresponding word on the master list. If he doesn't recognize the word, tell him and return the card to the pile, face down. Recognized cards are placed face up in another pile.

Continue as long as the child is interested or until all words have been recognized and are in the face up pile.

156. *Sound Grab Bag*

Make word cards, using words you think the child should recognize. Place the cards in a paper bag. Ask the youngster to reach into the bag and to tell you the word he "grabbed," and its beginning sound.

This is an excellent review exercise, and one which gives you an accurate evaluation of your child's knowledge. Add new words to the collection as he masters them.

157. *Word Hide And Seek*

To promote rapid scanning of reading material, ask your child to search through a book and to locate as many words as possible with a certain beginning sound. Ask him to print the words as he locates them, and at the end of the specified time, have him read them back to you. (Help him with the ones he doesn't know.)

158. *Which Word Doesn't Belong?*

To help the child hear beginning sounds, say three or four words and ask him to identify the one which doesn't begin with the same sound as the others.

Examples:

    dog   deer   dinner   car
    shut   bridge   shoe   shell

159. *I'm Thinking*
You start the game by saying, "I'm thinking of something in the room that starts like "father." Can you guess what it is?"

The child might say, "Is it the funnies?"

You reply, "No, it isn't the funnies, but it has the same sound."

He continues guessing objects which begin with the *f* sound. If he guesses an object which does not have the proper beginning sound, mention this fact to him. At last he'll say, "Is it the fireplace?"

You reply, "Yes, it is the fireplace."

The child now becomes the leader and chooses an object and sound for you to guess.

160. *A Rhyming Guessing Game*
You say, "This is a rhyming guessing game. Guess what I'm thinking."

    a. I'm thinking of a color that rhymes with <u>chew</u>. (blue)
    b. I'm thinking of a water animal that rhymes with <u>pail</u>. (whale)
    c. I'm thinking of a color that rhymes with <u>tack.</u> (black)
    d. I'm thinking of something to play with that rhymes with <u>boy</u>. (toy)
    e. I'm thinking of something to wear that rhymes with <u>rat.</u> (hat)
    f. I'm thinking of a place to swim that rhymes with <u>cake.</u> (lake)
    g. I'm thinking of a kind of tree that rhymes with <u>smoke</u>. (oak)
    h. I'm thinking of a small gray animal that rhymes with <u>house.</u> (mouse)
    i. I'm thinking of a smart animal that rhymes with <u>box</u>. (fox)
    j. I'm thinking of a large animal that rhymes with <u>goose.</u> (moose)

161. *I Can Spell!*
When the child has learned to use phonics, he'll enjoy spelling. Start by thinking of rhyming words such as cat, hat, rat, fat, bat, mat, pat, sat, etc.

You would explain, "If cat is c-a-t, how do you think you'd spell hat?" If he doesn't understand, tell him the "at" will sound the same each time. If he has mastered the sounds of the beginning consonants, he'll have no problem in spelling the above words, and he'll be pleased at how "smart" he is.

Other easy word families which will provide practice for him in using his phonics to good advantage are the following:
    ook (book, cook, hook, look, nook)
    it (hit, bit, fit, lit, mit, pit, sit, wit)
    ar (car, bar, far, jar, mar, par)

162. Word Families And Blends

To provide practice in recognizing rhyming words and in using consonant blends, try the following exercise.

a. With a magic marker print twelve common word endings in the twelve divisions of an egg carton. Endings might be: ing, at, it, ight, ack, ar, in, all, ig, ick, ill, ell, or any others with which the child needs practice.

Print three words for each ending. For "ing," you might have king, sing, ring and for "at," cat, fat, bat, etc. Cut the words apart and place them face down. Have the child pick up a card, pronounce it and then place it in the proper compartment in the egg carton.

b. A variation of the above game is to use twelve blends. (Bl, pl, br, gr, st, sm, wh, sp, ch, wh, sk, sh, etc.) Words used in this variation would not rhyme but would begin with the blends you have printed in the carton as: black, blink, blue, etc.

163. Practice With Word Endings

The child now is aware that words with the same ending belong to a word family. Pronounce four words, three of which belong to the same family, and suggest that he tell which one doesn't belong.

wink	think	long	brink
bank	jar	crank	thank
not	saw	jaw	law
five	hive	dive	my
catch	hatch	box	match

164. Word Family Book

Constructing a word family book may be a challenging activity for your child. Have him staple together about forty pages of paper. He may wish to decorate the cover of his book.

Suggest that he use one page for each word family. Have him place the ending for the page at the top. Suggested endings are:
ink   ack   ank   ook   ide   ake   eat   ight   atch   ing   ew   oo
aw   all   ur   ar   or   ow   ou   ay   oy   ose   ink   ong
old   end   ate   it   ark   and   et   ame   ang   oat   ear   ound
ought

Have him "try on" various consonants and consonant blends until he builds words. (See Exercise 149 for several blends.) Ask him to read his list when he has completed a family.

Warning! There is a tremendous amount of work in this exercise. Proceed slowly, distributing the assignments over many work periods. Properly used, this is a valuable activity. Improperly used, the child will be frustrated and discouraged.

165. *Using The Typewriter*

Use the typewriter as a teaching aid. Even small children can be taught the proper use of the machine so that it will not be damaged.

Suggestions:

a. Ask the young child to make a line of the various letters which you presently are teaching. Have him repeat the name of the letter each time he prints it.

b. Make capital and small letters for each symbol he has mastered, repeating the letter as he prints it.

c. Print as many words as he can recall from the word families with which he's acquainted. (See Exercise 164.)

d. Print his name and address.

e. Compose and print original "stories." (Three or four word sentences with your help in spelling.)

166. *Around And Around We Go*

This exercise gives practice in hearing and using suffixes (word endings). Make a wheel from cardboard. Print word endings near the outside. Fasten a hand to the center with a metal fastener. As the child spins the wheel have him think of words that end with the suffix at which the spinner stops.

Examples:

Walking, slowly, faster, slowest, boys, pushed, etc.

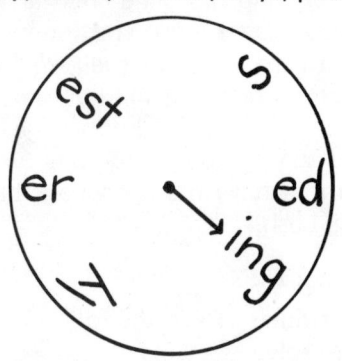

167. *A Sound Wheel*

This device will give the child practice in combining beginning and ending sounds in the formation of words. Make a cardboard wheel as illustrated from two pieces of cardboard, one approximately twelve inches in diameter and the other about ten inches in size. Fasten the wheels together with a metal fastener.

Construct the device so that both easy and difficult blends and endings are used. (See Exercises 149 and 162.) As the child spins the wheel have him try to pronounce the words he forms.

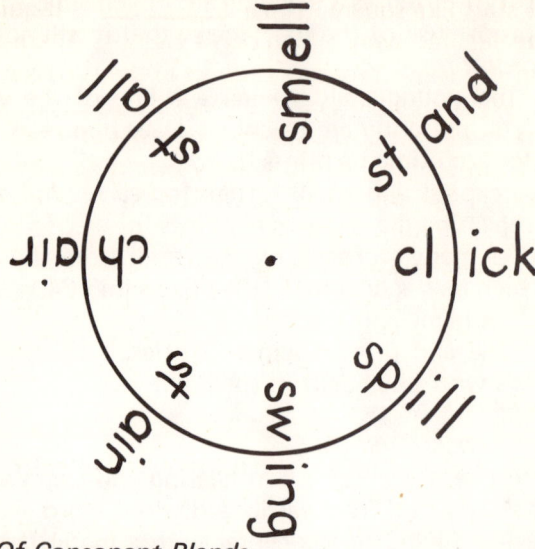

(wheel diagram with blends/endings: smell, stand, click, spill, swing, stair, ch air, ts oll)

168. *Review Of Consonant Blends*

Occasionally you'll need an accurate evaluation of the extent of the child's knowledge of consonant blends. Make a few cards on which you print the blends you wish to evaluate. Perhaps you've selected *sp, sh, sm, gr,* and *br.* The child arranges the blend cards before him, and as you say a word starting with one of the blends, he selects the correct card. (*Sp* for spell, *sh* for shoe, *gr* for grow.)

Select some words which the child does not readily recognize as a check on his skill in applying his knowledge of phonics. (You can easily find words in the dictionary for this type of exercise.) Also include some words that have the consonant blend in the middle, or at the end. (Pu<u>sh</u>ing, bu<u>sh</u>.)

169. *Riddles With Sounds*

Children enjoy riddles. Read the following, or make up original ones for your child to solve.

a. I am on a building. Sometimes I'm very high. I'm made of metal. I help your TV get a good picture. I start like apple. I'm an _____. (Antenna)

b. I'm a bird. People think I'm very wise. I make scary sounds at night. I sleep in the day. I rhyme with howl. I'm an _____. (Owl)

c. You see me in the daytime. I'm large, bright and hot. I help

plants grow. People never visit me because I'm very hot and far away. I rhyme with fun. I'm the _____ . (Sun)
d. I'm a furry animal with a bushy tail. I live in trees and eat nuts. I start like square. I'm a _____ . (Squirrel)
e. We're far, far away. Men don't visit us. There are thousands of us in the sky. You can't see us in the daytime or on cloudy nights. We rhyme with cars. We are _____ . (Stars)
f. We're made of paper. We may be large or small. People learn things from looking at us. Nearly everyone uses us. We rhyme with cooks. We are _____ . (Books)

170. *Finding Little Words In Big Words*
Print words which are familiar to the child. Ask him to search for little words within the big word. Some words may contain several little words. Have him circle all he can see.
Examples:

bigger	faster	tent	cookies	himself
window	everything	Saturday	unhappy	answer
return	stopped	beside	small	teacher
together	someone	thinking	however	reading

171. *Word Games*
Word games stimulate the child's thinking and give additional practice in phonics.
a. Ask the child to name all the objects he can see that start with a certain letter or sound in two minutes.
Example:
    Door, dog, dish, davenport, doll.
b. Suggest that he try to think of a word which rhymes with another, and then to make up a short jingle using the rhyming words.
Examples:

    (bird, heard)   (floor pour)
    I thought I heard   Baby will pour
    An early bird.   Milk on the floor.

172. *Scrambled Words*
Children will find this activity great fun if it is kept at their level of maturity. From a list of easy words which the child knows, "scramble" the letters. Ask the youngster to unscramble them and to print the word correctly. As a clue, the capital is the first letter of the word.

Examples:
   Cat might be "taC, atC or aCt"
   All might be "lAl or llA"
   See might be "eSe, or eeS"

173. *Rhymes And Riddles*
   a. Change a letter in <u>round</u> and you have a kind of dog. (hound)
   Change a letter in <u>spring</u> and you'll have a cord. (string)
   Change a letter in <u>pan</u> and you'll have a person. (man)
   Change a letter in <u>see</u> and you'll have an insect. (bee)
   Change a letter in <u>hair</u> and you'll have two of something. (pair)
   Change a letter in <u>day</u> and you'll have a month. (May)
   Change a letter in <u>men</u> and you'll have something that writes. (pen)
   Change a letter in <u>walk</u> and you'll have something else people can do. (talk)

   b. Using the pairs of rhyming words from the above exercise, see if the child can make two line jingles, as:
   My new <u>ball</u>   A big brown <u>hound</u>
   Rolled down the <u>hall.</u>   Ran round and <u>round.</u>

   c. Still another way to encourage the child to listen for and to compose rhymes is to say something like: "I know a boy who has a toy. Can you hear the rhyming words?" (boy toy)

   Choose another word such as fox. Say, "Can you think of something that rhymes with fox?" He might say, "box."

   Suggest that he make a rhyme using fox and box. He might say, "I see a fox in a box."

   Other pairs of words you might suggest for rhyming include:

owl	howl	frog	log
tree	three	Mother	brother
flag	bag	mouse	house
sun	fun	me	flea

   Print the child's rhymes as he composes them. He'll enjoy reading his "poetry." (Give him help on words when necessary.)

174. *Find The Mates*
   To stimulate the child's thinking and to increase his vocabulary you can print pairs of words or groups of words, which have nearly the same meaning. Cut them apart and ask the child to find the mates.
   Examples:

two of something	a pair	begin	started
all at once	suddenly	house	home
fastened	tied	stone	rock
go after	follow	slick	slippery

175. *Scrambled Sentences And Stories*
   Children like the challenge of unscrambling stories, if the work is not too difficult. In manuscript printing, make a two or three sentence story. Print each sentence in a different color. (Sentence one could be in red, sentence two in blue and sentence three in green.)
   Cut the sentences into individual words. To assemble the story the child will first place all words of each color in separate piles. Second, he will reassemble the sentences, and last he will place the sentences in the proper sequence to make a story.
   Vary the difficulty of the sentences with the child's reading ability.
   Examples:
   a. Kittens are baby cats. Puppies are baby dogs. Kittens and puppies do not open their eyes until they are several days old.
   b. Camels live in the desert. Camels can go many days without drinking water.
   c. We live in the United States. There are fifty states in the United States.
   Variations:
   Tell the child there is a surprise in a scrambled sentence, as: We will go to the zoo this afternoon.
   Compliment him on something he has done well, as:
   Your room is very neat today.

176. *Words That Have More Than One Meaning (Homonyms)*
   Explain to the child that homonyms are words that sound alike when we say them, but that they have more than one meaning. Use the word casually in conversation as you talk of this exercise.
   Ask the child to use the following homonyms in the sentences. You likely will teach only one or two homonyms at a time.
   Common homonyms include: to, too, two; here, hear; knows, nose; their, there.
   a. Bobby's dog, Jack _____ the way home. He follows his _____ .
   b. Jane and her sister went _____ the store. She spent her_____ dimes. Her little sister spent her money, _____.
   c. Mother called again, "Carl! Come _____! Didn't you _____ me call you before?"
   d. Mrs. Smith said, "The children may put _____ coats over _____ in that closet."

177. *The Bookworm*
   Children who enjoy stories will like to see their bookworm grow. Suggest that the more stories he eats, the faster he grows.

Make the bookworm's head from green paper and put it up in a prominent spot. Each time a new book is read, add a segment with the name of the book printed on it.

Both toddlers and children who read independently will be interested in watching their bookworm get longer.

178. *Primary Word Lists*

If you would feel more comfortable in using a standard primary word list, there are numerous good ones. These lists consist of from 500 to 1,000 words which are most commonly used in daily living and are among the ones taught in primary reading. A primary teacher in your school, or the school librarian, could suggest the ones used in your school.

We are not including primary word lists because we believe that if children learn basic reading skills and methods of attacking new words, such a list is unnecessary, since the child will learn new words as he has a need for them.

Arithmetic (Reread Chapter Six, pages 37 to 39.)

179. *Counting And Identifying Numerals*

a. Teach your toddler to count by using familiar objects which he can handle—crayons, blocks, books and toys. Have him touch each one as he counts it.

Use numbers in your conversation with him, as "You have four trucks," or "You'll be three your next birthday." While getting lunch you might say,"We use two slices of bread to make a sandwich."

b. In teaching numbers, teach the meaning of "zero." You might say, "There are zero elephants in our yard. Zero means "not any." Continue with other statements as, "There are zero puppies in your toy box," etc.

c. When the child shows a desire to make the numerals you might place them from 0 to 9 on his chalkboard or on paper. The numerals should be large, probably about two or three inches in height. Have the child trace over them with his middle or index finger.

Large sandpaper numerals mounted on cardboard are du[rable and] effective for "finger tracing."

180. *In The Middle*
To teach the meaning of "in the middle," show the child three of many types of objects—dishes, doors, pictures, toys, trinkets, chairs, books, etc. Point out the middle object and explain the meaning of the term. Rearrange the three objects in the group and ask him to select the middle one. Continue the exercise until the child grasps the concept.

181. *Comparisons*
Show the child two objects of different sizes. Ask him to point out the larger one. Now, using the same two objects, ask him to point out the smaller one. Use the terms "larger" and "smaller" in conversation with him.

Suitable objects for comparison are books, oranges, apples, pencils, crayons, shoes, coats, pictures, etc.

182. *How Many?*
a. To teach counting as well as an understanding of numbers, knock slowly on the table and ask the youngster to count the knocks aloud.
b. Ask him to take a certain number of steps, counting aloud as he walks.
c. Count objects of interest while driving in the car. (Trucks, schools, certain colors of cars, stop lights, etc.)

183. *Teaching Numerals (A Quiet Play Activity)*
Make large numerals in marked-off squares on a shirt cardboard. In the beginning use only three or four numerals as:

1	2
3	4

Pretend the numerals represent houses. Ask the child how quickly he can get to house 2. Have him place his finger on it. Continue visiting other houses.

Add more numerals when he has mastered the first ones taught, but review the old ones often.

...g Numbers

...little value to the child if he recognizes numerals ...anding of number. To help him grasp the meaning ...or tie together eleven large pieces of paper. Make ...rough 10 with one page devoted to each numeral. ...how the meaning of each numeral as:

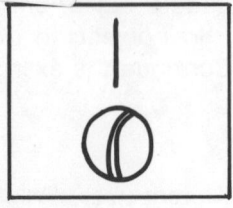

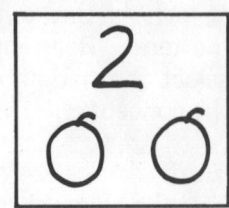

185. *Flannelboard Exercises*

You can make numbers and shapes meaningful and provide the child with enjoyable activities by often using the flannelboard. (See Exercise 41.)

Suggestions:

a. Cut felt or construction paper petals (nine or ten) and a circular center which may be arranged to form a daisy.

Ask the child to form a flower on the flannelboard by using any number of petals he wishes. Have him count the petals he used. After he makes several flowers with varying numbers of petals, suggest that he draw and color the daisies. Write the number of petals below each one.

b. Cut pairs of felt or construction paper circles, one large and the other small, using several colors. Compare the size of the circles so the child is aware that there is a large and small circle of each color. Place all but one circle on the flannelboard. Ask, "What is missing?" (He'd answer, "The large red circle," etc.)

When he does this activity easily proceed in the same way to squares, triangles and rectangles.

186. *Likenesses and Differences*

a. This activity helps children to see likenesses and differences which is a skill necessary to success in many academic areas, including arithmetic and reading. To prepare the work, make two or three simple objects in a row. Make them alike except for a minor missing detail on one object. Ask the child to find what is missing and to complete the picture as:

b. Sorting objects teaches observation and helps a child to see likenesses and differences.

Give him a box containing your old buttons. Have him sort them in many ways as: old and new; by color; two hole or four hole; plastic, metal, wood or pearl; bright or dull.

187. *Which Numerals Are Missing?*
Make number cards from one to ten. Place them in order on the floor or table. Ask the child to cover his eyes. Remove one card. Ask, "Which numeral is missing?" When he is able to do more difficult work, remove two cards and have him find which ones are missing.

Other activities which you may carry out with these cards are to mix them so they are not in order, and have the child arrange them correctly. When this work becomes easy, mix the cards and remove one or two. Ask, "Which numerals are missing?"

188. *Follow The Dots*
Arrange numerals so that when they are connected in the correct order the child will see a recognizable figure or shape. Have him connect the dots.

189. *Number Puzzles*
a. Cut cardboard into uniform 5 x 7 inch sizes. With a magic marker write a numeral on the left half of the card. On the right half, draw or paste a corresponding number of objects.

Cut the card between the numeral and picture to make a two piece puzzle. Make a two piece puzzle for each numeral you wish to teach, attempting to cut each one so that none except the correct match will fit.

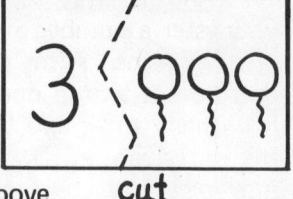

b. Teach number combinations as in *a* above.

Another idea is to cut all similar sums or differences so that the sums are interchangeable as: 2 + 2 = 4, 3 + 1 = 4, 1 + 3 = 4, 0 + 4 = 4, 4 + 0 = 4. All of the answers (4) will fit any of the combinations.

190. *Recognizing Numerals And Color Words*

The objective of this dual purpose exercise is to have the child learn color words and to use numerals as he crayons an attractive design.

On a large piece of paper make a design containing numerals which your child recognizes. Make a color chart with corresponding numerals as follows: All of the "1" sections will be crayoned red, the "2's" green, etc. To assist the child in reading color words, place a dot of the correct color following the word as:

1 red o
2 green o
3 yellow o
4 blue o
5 orange o
6 brown o
7 black o
8 purple o

191. *Introducing The Addition And Subtraction Concepts*

Gradually through conversation you'll introduce the concept of addition. "If we put this spoon with these two spoons, we'll have three spoons in all," or, "You have two pairs of shoes in the closet. How many shoes are there?"

Another way to introduce the addition concept is to give the youngster a number of objects which is less than ten. (Try chocolate bits or raisins. After a few minutes work, he can eat them.) Suggest that he put two in one pile and three in another, then count to see how many three and two are. Use the words "plus" and "equal" in the conversation. Don't expect an automatic answer, but encourage him to count to find the sums. The important point is that he understands that when two groups are put together, the result is more than either single group.

The subtraction concept may be introduced using the same approach, except that he "takes away" the smaller number of objects from the larger.

192. *Teaching Addition And Subtraction Concepts*
To help the child understand the meaning of addition and subtraction, the following suggestions are effective.
   a. Use 3 x 5 unlined index cards or cut cardboard into uniform sizes. Draw simple pictures of objects on one side with the number word beneath. On the opposite side of the card make the corresponding numeral as:

front	back	front	back
⓪ ⓪ ⓪ three	3	⓪ ⓪ two	2

Ask the child how many apples he'd have if he had three apples and two apples. Show him the pictures, and have him count them. Turn the cards to the numeral side. Tell him the numerals mean the same number as the pictures, (3 + 2) and that we can also write it as 3 + 2 = 5. Use plus (+) and minus (-) signs.

This procedure may be followed with any addition or subtraction combination you wish to teach. Vary the pictures on cards to maintain interest. And again, it is more important that the child understands that when groups of objects are put together, he gets more, and when some are taken away, he gets less, than that his response is automatic. Encourage him to count to find sums using number cards, bottle caps, crayons, blocks, buttons, or any objects which interest him in gaining the addition and subtraction concepts.

193. *How Many?*
In this exercise we still are emphasizing the meaning of addition—that when two groups are put together, we get more.

To make a game of addition, use a spinner from one of your child's games in which the numerals do not go higher than five or six. Spin the hand two times, saying aloud the numerals on which the hand stopped, as "four and two. How many are four and two?"

Give the child sufficient time to find the sums in any way he wishes—by making marks, counting on his fingers, counting two crayons and four crayons, etc.

194. *Making Comparisons*
   Adjust the material to your child's level of ability.
   a. Show two objects of differing size, (books, balls, dolls) and ask, "Which is less? More? Larger? Smaller? Higher? Heavier?
   b. Ask, "Which is more?" — Five girls or three girls? Six balls or ten balls? Seven apples or five apples? Ten boys or nineteen boys?
   c. Ask, "Which is less?" — Eleven houses or nine houses? Ten crayons or twelve crayons? Eight hot dogs or six hot dogs? Eleven dolls or ten dolls? Fifteen cents or ten cents? A quarter or a dime? A dollar or fifty cents?
   d. Ask, "Which is heavier?" — A boy or a horse? A cow or a pig? A mouse or a kitten?
   e. Ask, "Which is higher?" A cloud or a tree? A house or a skyscraper? A telephone pole or a bus?
   f. Ask, "Which is smaller?" A bird or a dog? A cat or a fox? A bus or a car?

195. *Learning About Money*
   Teach your child the names of various pieces of money. Using coins from his allowance or bank, teach the penny, nickel. dime, quarter and half dollar. Proceed as long as he shows interest and grasps the concepts.
   Matching games using coins are an effective method of teaching money. *Example:* A nickel will buy as much as five pennies; a quarter is equal to two dimes and a nickel, or five nickels, or twenty-five pennies.
   A word of warning! Do not hold the child to long tiring assignments or discussions. Stop immediately when he shows lack of interest or indicates the material may be too difficult to be meaningful.

196. *Telling Time*
   When a child is able to read numerals it is not difficult to teach him to tell time by the hour and half hour. If he is able to reach this stage in telling time, it will simplify the bedtime decision as well as snacks too close to mealtime.

197. *Make The Set Match The Numeral*
    (Reread "Sets," Chapter Six, page 38.)
    To help the child understand the relationship between objects and numerals, draw pictures of incomplete sets and put a numeral in the box indicating the number of objects desired. Ask the child to complete the set.
    Examples:
    a.

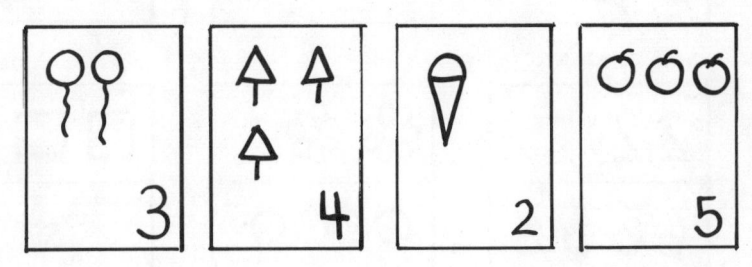

♀♀	↑ ↑ ↑	▽	◊◊◊
3	4	2	5

    b. Write the numeral that tells how many are in the set.

✿✿ ✿	MM	▫▫▫ ▫▫	◊◊ ◊◊

    c. As you and your child go about your daily life, suggest often that he count various items such as toys, cars, children, animals, stores, houses, etc.
    d. Play, "I See A Set." You can start the game by saying, "I see a set of two." (Might be doors, dresses, shoes, etc.) The child now has three guesses. When he guesses correctly, he is "it," and the game continues with you guessing the set he has in mind.

198. *Equivalent Sets*
    To teach the meaning of the term equivalent, make several sets from toys and suggest that the child make them equivalent. If the term is new to him, explain that he will have the same number in each of two sets if they are equivalent.
    Examples:
    a. Three blocks and three cars
       Four trucks and four books
       Five dolls and five dresses

b. Draw unequal sets and ask the child to make them equivalent.

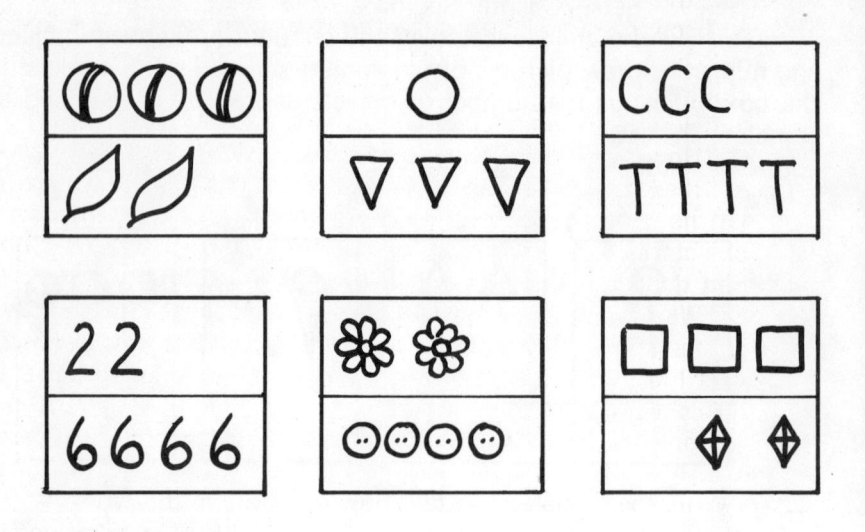

199. *Odd, Even And Equal*
a. When the child can count and identify numerals from 0 to 9, cut off and discard three compartments from an egg carton. Give him forty-five small objects such as buttons, beans or raisins and ask him to put the same number of objects in each compartment. Ask how many he has in each section. There should be five. Say, "There is an equal number in each compartment—each one has five."

b. To teach the concept of odd and even, give the child a number of objects and ask him to place them in pairs. If none are left, he started with an even number, and if one is left, he started with an odd number of objects.

Another suggestion for teaching this concept is to draw a large number of circles, squares, or triangles on a sheet of paper. Ask the child to draw circles around each pair. See if he can decide whether there were an even or odd number of figures on the page.

200. *Meaningful Numbers*
Numbers should be taught through application to the child's everyday life. Make numbers have meaning for him. Suppose you are planning a party for his fifth birthday. He has invited five children, three boys and two girls. How might you use the occasion to teach numbers in a meaningful way?

Suggestions:
Ask the child:
a. "How many children do we need to plan for?" (3 + 2 = 5)
b. "Did you forget yourself?" (5 + 1 = 6) "There will be 6 children."
c. "How many places will we set at the table?" (6)
d. "How many children will sit on each side?" (3. 3 + 3 = 6)
e. "If each child has 2 cookies, how many cookies will we need?" (If the child needs help give him buttons, raisins or other small objects to aid him in figuring out the number needed.) Show him that he is thinking out how much 6 + 6 are.)
f. "We have only 4 astronaut glasses, so we'll use Mickey Mouse glasses to fill in. How many Mickey Mouse glasses will we need?" (Let him figure it out. Only if he needs help show him that he needs two.)
Continue in this manner with other plans for the party.

201. *Using The Number Line*

The number line will help the child to quickly solve addition and subtraction problems. (See explanation of the number line on page 39, Chapter 6.) Later you may make the numerals as high as you wish, but when the child is learning to use the number line it is best to go no higher than 10.

```
0   1   2   3   4   5   6   7   8   9   10
|___|___|___|___|___|___|___|___|___|___|
```

Teach the child to use the number line by using simple combinations. Show him how to find sums and differences. (Use these terms when working with him, explaining as often as necessary that the answer to an addition combination is called a "sum," and the answer to a subtraction problem is called the "difference.")

Ask the child to solve "story problems" by using the number line.

Examples:
a. At Jimmy's party there were 5 boys and 5 girls. How many children were at his party?
b. Three children left early. How many were still at the party?
c. They played 4 games before lunch and 3 games after lunch. How many games did they play at Jimmy's party?

Vary the difficulty of the problems with your child's ability. Make math fun—a part of his daily life. Use it as a game, a "see if you can find out" activity. Use blocks, beads, or other concrete objects to check answers he arrives at by using the number line. Stress the fact that in addition we "get more," and in subtraction we "get less."

202. *Addition and Subtraction Combinations*

The following combinations should be taught only as they have meaning for the child. Don't sit him down to memorize combinations, else he'll become bored, discouraged, and may come to dislike mathematics. Use these combinations when they can be applied to daily living. Remember to praise him when he is "smart" and figures out a new combination.

a. Addition Combinations (find the *sums)*

0 +0	8 +0	1 +7	3 +4	5 +4	1 +8	0 +1	7 +0	9 +0
9 +9	9 +8	8 +7	8 +8	8 +9	7 +8	9 +7	8 +6	7 +7
5 +0	0 +3	3 +1	3 +7	6 +2	1 +5	0 +4	3 +0	2 +3
6 +8	6 +7	5 +9	8 +5	7 +9	7 +6	9 +5	6 +6	5 +8
8 +4	5 +6	5 +5	4 +8	6 +5	3 +8	9 +2	7 +4	4 +2
2 +4	4 +3	7 +1	1 +2	0 +7	1 +1	2 +5	4 +4	7 +2
0 +8	8 +2	2 +6	4 +5	7 +3	0 +9	10 +0	2 +7	4 +6
8 +1	0 +10	5 +2	2 +8	5 +1	8 +2	1 +5	9 +1	3 +2
5 +2	9 +0	1 +6	3 +3	5 +3	1 +9	4 +6	5 +4	1 +1

b. Subtraction Combinations (find the *differences*)

0	3	4	6	8	10	1	4	4
−0	−1	−2	−6	−6	−2	−0	−1	−3

7	8	10	2	5	4	7	8	10
−1	−7	−3	−0	−1	−4	−2	−8	−4

9	17	18	15	16	17	15	16	14
−9	−9	−9	−8	−8	−8	−7	−7	−8

10	5	8	5	7	9	10	6	5
−6	−0	−1	−3	−5	−3	−7	−0	−4

7	9	10	7	10	5	7	9	10
−6	−4	−8	−0	−1	−5	−5	−5	−9

8	2	6	8	9	10	9	3	6
−0	−2	−1	−1	−6	−10	−0	−1	−2

14	14	13	14	13	16	13	14	12
−7	−6	−7	−5	−8	−9	−6	−9	−6

13	12	11	10	12	11	11	11	11
−5	−8	−5	−5	−4	−6	−3	−9	−7

2	4	1	5	8	6	9	3	7
−2	−3	−1	−3	−7	−4	−8	−2	−2

203. Put The Scales On The Fish

fish scale

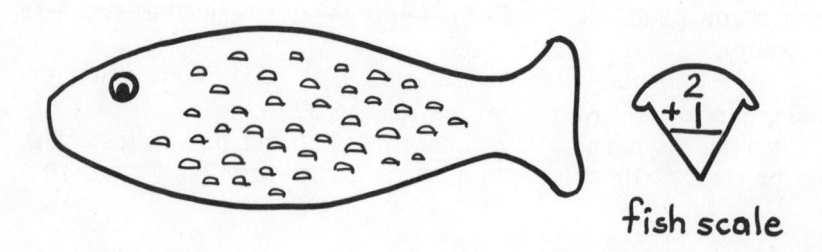

Draw a large fish on a piece of posterboard. Cut slots to hold the fish scales. Make the cone-shaped scales so the points will fit into the slots on the fish. Put a number combination on each scale.

As the child picks up a fish scale he says the combination and gives the answer. If correct, he puts the fish scale in a slot. If incorrect, he returns the scale to the bottom of the combination pile and continues with another. When the fish has all its scales, the game is completed.

Variations:
    Play the fish game to teach numerals, letters, shapes, colors, sounds or words.

204. "Arithmetic" Christmas Tree Ornaments

Draw and cut out a large construction paper evergreen tree. On white paper make ornaments of various shapes. Write number combinations on the white paper ornaments. Ask the child to color the ornaments in such a way that all combinations having the same answer are one color. (3 + 3, 4 + 2, 5 + 1, 0 + 6, 2 + 4, 1 + 5, and 6 + 0, all have 6 as the answer, so all would be colored the same. Combinations having 4 for an answer would be a different color, etc.)

Subtraction combinations may be included if the child has reached the level of maturity so that he readily changes from the addition to the subtraction process.

The ornaments are pasted on the Arithmetic Tree. You can accurately evaluate the child's knowledge of various combinations by his response to this fun activity.

205. Counting By 10

When the child has learned to count to 20, he will be eager to count to 100. You can clarify his understanding of the process if you prepare several groups of 10. You might use 10 groups of 10 toothpicks, each group fastened together with a rubber band.

Show him that two 10's (2 groups) are twenty. Have him count them aloud. In the discussion point out again that two 10's are twenty.

Show him how easily he can count to 30. Count aloud the three groups of 10 and say, "Three 10's are 30."

Proceed as long as he is interested in using the groups of 10, until he reaches 100. Have him count to 100 both by 1's and 10's.

206. *Tens And Ones*

Help the child to understand the importance of 10 in our number system. You likely will work with this concept several times before the child masters it completely. Don't hurry or pressure if he doesn't understand, but assure him that after a few more exercises, the concept will become clear.

a. Prepare several sets of 10. (Use toothpicks from exercise 205.) Ask, "How many are 2 tens? 4 tens? 6 tens? 10 tens?"

b. Separate one group of 10 toothpicks. Put individual toothpicks with groups of 10.

Example:

2 groups of 10 and 3 single toothpicks would represent 2 tens and 3 ones, or 23. Vary the groupings and ask the child to tell how many 10's and how many ones there are in:

22	(2 tens and 2 ones)	31	(3 tens and 1 one)
45		80	
78		54	
99		66	

Give as much practice as necessary, keeping work time brief if the concept is a difficult one for your child.

c. Make sets as follows on paper. Suggest that the child put an X under each set of 10.

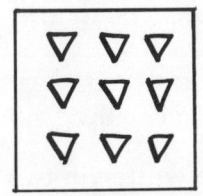

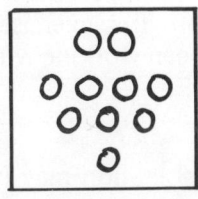

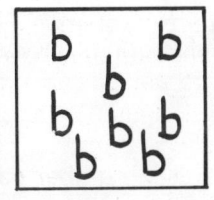

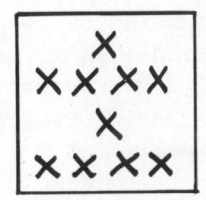

d. Ask the child to make 10 sets of 10.
e. Have him count objects in the 10 sets by 1's.

207. How Many Steps?
a. Suggest that the child guess how many steps it is to various places such as the refrigerator, to the door, to the bedroom, to the kitchen table, etc. Have him count aloud as he walks to find out whether he was correct.

b. Play "How Many Steps" outdoors. How many steps from the porch to the little tree? From the porch to the garage, etc.

208. Reading Numerals To 100
After the child has learned to count to 100 he will read the numerals quite easily. Show him that 66 is two 6's or 6 tens and 6 ones, and that the words almost tell him the numerals. (Exceptions are the 30's and 50's.)

Test his knowledge by giving him numerals to read. When he is confident, see if he can write numerals as you dictate them. Soon he will wish to write the numerals to 100.

209. Missing Numbers
As an evaluation activity prepare a worksheet as follows and ask the child to put in the missing numbers.

1 __ 3 __ __ 6 7 8 __ 10
__ __ 13 14 __ 16 __ 18 __ 20

210. How Numbers Grow
When the child reads and writes numbers easily he will enjoy making numbers grow. Buy a roll of paper that goes into an adding machine. Ask him to see how high he can go in writing numbers. If he asks, give help, otherwise do not interfere. He can roll his tape up as it grows.

The youngster will like to unroll the tape along the floor as he searches for certain numbers. From this exercise he will grow in understanding of the numbers he's been working with.

211. Twins
Explain that each number combination may be written in two ways as: 4 + 3 = 7, and

$$\begin{array}{r}4\\+3\\\hline 7\end{array}$$

a. Give each combination its twin and find the sums:

2 + 5 =   6 + 1 =   3 + 3 =   7 + 0 =

6 − 1 =   4 − 3 =   6 − 5 =   5 − 3 =

b. Write these combinations another way and find the answers:

3	4	2	0	7	5	9	8	1
−2	+4	+6	+7	−6	+4	−3	−7	+2

c. Prepare work as follows and ask the child to draw a line to the "twin," and to find the sums.

2 + 3 =   6 + 3 =   5 + 4 =   2 + 5 =

3 + 1 =   8 + 1 =   2 + 7 =

6	2	3	5	8	2	2
+3	+5	+1	+4	+1	+7	+3

212. *Learning About The Calendar*

Over an extended period of time you can teach your child the days of the week, and how to find the date on the calendar.

a. Point to various numbers on the calendar and demonstrate that they go from left to right, just as we read from left to right. Point to several, then give him dates to locate.

b. Show him where the days of the week are listed. Explain that dates in the column, below the day printed at the top, will fall on that specific day during the month.

c. Point out the month at the top of the page, and explain that there is usually a separate page for each month of the year.

d. Have the child repeat, in order, the days of the week. If he is unable to read them, have him say them in unison with you. Encourage him to memorize the days in the proper order.

e. Ask him to find certain dates as, Sunday, the 10th and Wednesday, the 27th.

213. *Ways Of Measuring*

Talk of measuring other things besides time. Discuss distance, which is measured in miles, liquids which are measured by cups, pints, quarts and gallons, temperature which is measured by degrees, a person's height which is measured by feet and inches and the day which is measured by hours. He may think of others including the year which is measured by days, weeks, and months.

You will readily recognize the great amount of material covered by the term "measuring." Teach the child the measurement terms for which he has a need, is interested in, and can comprehend.

Choose from the exercises below, the ones most helpful to the child.

    a. Use inch, foot, yard, mile. What would you use to measure a desk? a book? the size of your room? the size of our lawn?
    b. How is the distance between cities measured? Have the youngster measure things about the home using a foot ruler and yardstick.
    c. What would you use to measure the following? (Use pound, dozen, quart, peck, yard.) Cheese, potatoes, cloth, eggs, carrots, milk, sugar, doughnuts.

214. *Measuring Time*

After the child has learned to use the calendar, teach him the months. Use a calendar with large print and numerals. Starting with January, say the names of the months in order as you turn the pages. Repeat, and ask him to say the months with you. Continue as long as he is interested. After a few brief work periods, he likely will have memorized the months in order.

Talk of holidays, changes in weather and activities in the various months. Pinpoint family birthdays, perhaps circling them on the calendar.

    a. If the child is reading easily, ask him to use the calendar to fill the following blanks. Perhaps he'd like to memorize the rhyme when he has correctly filled the blanks.

>Thirty days have September,
>April, June and _____ ,
>All the rest have thirty-one
>Except _____ , which alone
>Has twenty-eight,
>But one day more
>We add to it each year in four.

Explain leap year. This explanation can lead into a science discussion about the solar system, the earth's orbit and reasons for our seasons.

b. Have the child use the calendar to find answers to these questions:

> When is your birthday? Find it on the calendar. What day does it come on this year?
> How many months are there in a year? Name them.
> In what month is Thanksgiving? Christmas? Halloween? Fourth of July? Memorial Day?
> What is the first month of the year? The last month?
> Which are the hot summer months? the cold winter months?
> Which are the spring months? the fall months?

General Knowledge

Encourage your child to ask "Why?" when he doesn't understand something he observes. Give him information appropriate to his ability of understanding. And don't sell him short. He probably is capable of greater comprehension than you've thought.

215. *Teaching Cause And Effect*
Your toddler can be taught to live comfortably and safely within his immediate environment if you'll explain, and sometimes demonstrate, the results of certain activities.
Examples:
a. "I'm sorry you pinched your finger. Next time take your other hand away when you close the door."
b. "If you stand under the table you'll bump your head. You're taller than the table."
c. "Food grinders can grind fingers just the way they grind meat."
d. "I must be very careful for I'm using a sharp knife."
e. "If it doesn't rain this afternoon, we'll water the flowers tonight."
Such explanations teach a child to think about cause and effect and help him to be alert to danger and more obedient to necessary rules.

216. *Short Trips Teach A Child*
To increase the child's knowledge about the world outside the home you should take him on short trips.
Suggestions:
a. Take him to the farm or the zoo. Take time to talk about the animals. When it is permitted, allow him to pet the friendly

ones. If he can sit on a pony's back, feel the sleek coat, watch the pony eat, hear him neigh, and smell the barn odors your child is learning through all his senses.
b. Take walks about the back yard or in the park. Watch the insects—ants, bees, butterflies, flies, grasshoppers, and crickets. Point out a bird catching insects and explain how she feeds her little ones. Perhaps you'll find a bird's nest.
c. Take a short bus or train trip. The child will love it!
d. Visit a greenhouse or an orchard. Show him the growing plants and fruit.
e. Take a trip to the fire station. Let him talk to the firemen. Perhaps he may sit on the firetruck.
f. Go to the beach. Gather pebbles and shells.

217. *Knowledge Games*
Games are fun as well as educational. They may be used to occupy your child's mind while you're going about your housework, as well as at quiet times.
Suggestions:
a. Think of rhyming words. (chair, hair, fair; ball, hall, fall)
b. How many red things can you see? green? etc.
c. How many kinds of furniture are in our house?
d. How many kinds of fruit can you think of? vegetables? meat? animals? birds? cars? trucks? dogs? (You wouldn't use all of these at one work time.)
e. How many relatives' names can you remember? friends?

218. *Which One Doesn't Belong?*
Make a series of pictures with one which doesn't fit the classification of the others, as, 3 kinds of fruit and 1 bird. Ask the child to identify the one that doesn't belong with the others and have him give his reason for the answer. (All of the pictures are fruit except the bird, so he doesn't belong.)
Suggestions:
a. Make 3 or 4 pictures of objects belonging to the same classification, with one which doesn't belong, as:
  Vegetables: (radish, lettuce, carrot, etc.,) and a building
  People: (boy, girl, man) and a tree
  Flowers and a vegetable
  Electrical appliances and a book
  Manufactured items and a living plant or animal
  Land animals and a water animal
  Letters and a numeral

Letters and a figure (triangle, rectangle, square, circle)
Capital letters and a small letter
Toys and a full size tractor

b. The above order may be reversed, as, 3 buildings and a vegetable, etc. throughout suggestions in *a.* above.

c. As the child matures, pictures may not be necessary. You may say, "I saw a duck, a fox, an airplane and a boy. Which one doesn't belong? (The airplane, since it's not alive.)

Other Suggestions:

cat	dog	horse	bluejay
girl	boy	house	man
pine	car	maple	oak
truck	chair	table	sofa
pencil	paper	crayon	pen
book	cake	pie	cookies
red	green	tree	blue
window	flower	door	floor
lamp	lantern	sun	telephone
robin	bluebird	canary	turtle
pork	beef	candy	lamb

You'll think of many more!

219. *Neighborhood Map*

To lay the foundation for an understanding of maps, help the child make a map of your block putting in the street and houses. Mark north, south, east and west on the map and explain that north is always toward the top, south toward the bottom, east to the right and west to the left of the map. Your child may wish to put in trees and other places of special interest to him.

220. *Hurry!*

Explain that you will race with the clock. Take turns seeing how many correct objects you can name in one minute. Use only one or two categories at a work period.

Categories might be:

Boys' names
Girls' names
Kinds of fruit
Kinds of vegetables
Kinds of birds
Kinds of cars
Domestic animals
Wild animals
Kinds of dogs
Kinds of trees
Kinds of flowers
Kinds of meats
Things that fly
Things that make music
Things that run
Kinds of insects

221. Who Am I? (Riddles)
This exercise stimulates the child's awareness of community helpers. You say:

a. I help people who are in trouble. I try to stop people from doing things which would harm someone. I wear a uniform and a badge. Who am I? (Policeman)

b. I ride on a red truck that goes very fast. Sirens shriek and bells ring when I'm on the speeding truck. Other men are on the truck, too. We are hurrying to help someone in trouble. We must get there as soon as possible. I put on a slicker and rain hat so I'll be ready when we stop. I'm a _____ . (Fireman)

c. I carry a big bag. I leave letters and magazines at houses. I walk past the same houses every day whether the weather is good or bad. I don't always stop at every house. I'm a _____ . (Postman)

d. Continue with other community helpers such as teachers, school principal, milkman, garbage man, postmaster, etc. Depending upon your child's maturity, he may like to compose riddles about community helpers as you take turns playing the various roles while the other guesses who he is imitating.

222. How People Travel
a. Ask the child to name as many ways of travel as he can. List them as he thinks of them. If this is a new concept, you may need to give him clues.

Examples:

car	bus	truck	train
airplane	helicopter	jet	boat
ship	canoe	snowmobile	horse
dog sled	walking	motorcycle	bike
spaceship	scooter		

b. Introduce the word "transportation." Ask how many methods of transportation he can recall from the above list.

Have the child draw pictures illustrating his favorite methods of transportation.

223. Traffic Safety
Discuss safety as you walk with the child on the sidewalk beside a busy street. When crossing the street, teach him to observe the traffic light and to walk only with the green light. Talk about and teach him to recognize the more common traffic signs. Stress the fact that pedestrians must not only observe and follow traffic rules

and regulations but they must be mentally alert and quick to size up emergency situations and to make sound, safe decisions.

Talk about walking on a road where there is no sidewalk. Stress the fact that in such a situation we walk on the left shoulder of the road, facing traffic, so that we can see approaching cars, and that we cross the street only at crosswalks.

Bicyclists also must obey the traffic rules of the road. The rider must realize that he has a responsibility for his own safety, and that he should ride as near the right hand side of the road as possible. Point out the careless bike rider and the danger he is placing himself in.

Talk to the youngster about the function of the school safety patrol. Teach him to respect the safety boys.

Help the child to understand what he, as a pedestrian now, and as a bike rider or automobile driver later, can do to protect himself and others in present day traffic.

224. *Thinking Of The Future*

Children need to be guided to plan for the future in a "let's pretend" sort of way. You can help your child to think of future possibilities by leading his thoughts through an imaginative exploration of issues which may sometime confront him.

Examples:

a. Imagine you are ten years old. What will you and your friends like to play? When you are ten, how old will your friends be? How old will your brother and sister be?

b. Imagine you are nine years old. What will you like to read about? What kind of TV programs will you like? Will they be the same ones you enjoy now? Why, or why not?

c. Imagine you are fifteen years old. Will you still be in high school? Will you work after school and in the summer to earn money for things you want? What kind of work would you like?

d. Imagine you have graduated from college. What kind of work would you like to do? About how old will you be? What will your mother and father be doing? (Remember they'll be older, too.)

225. *Categories*

This exercise gives the child practice in categorizing. Prepare a list similar to the following and suggest that he place 1 line under things we ride in, or on, and 2 lines under words that mean money.

a.
airplane	car	train	bob sled
scooter	truck	bicycle	trailer
dime	tractor	quarter	penny
dollar	skis	nickel	streetcar
boat	half dollar	skates	sled
bus	cent	wagon	subway
engine	dime	ship	cart
jet	motorboat		

b. Put 1 after words that mean people.
Put 2 after words that mean countries.
Put 3 after words that are things to wear.

uncle	aunt	Japan	children
farmer	gloves	England	sister
shoes	lady	Ireland	United States
hat	coat	mittens	teacher
men	gloves	woman	cap
mother	Germany	Mexico	China
James	brother	Italy	shirt
raincoat	Egypt		

Bibliography And Suggested Readings

Arnold, Arnold. *Violence And Your Child,* Award Books, 1969.
Ashley, Rosalind Minor. *Successful Techniques For Teaching Elementary Language Arts,* Parker Publishing, 1970.
Beck, Joan. *How To Raise A Brighter Child,* Trident Press, 1969.
Beecher, Marguerite and Willard. *Parents On The Run,* Matrix House, Ltd.
Chappel, Bernice M. *Independent Learning Activities,* 1973; *Language Arts Seatwork For Primary Grades,* Fearon Publishers, 1967.
Chappel, Bernice M. *Listening And Learning,* Fearon Publishers, 1973.
Chappel, Bernice M. *Mathematics Seatwork For Primary Grades,* Fearon Publishers, 1970.
Cline and Ishee. "Specific Learning Disabilities." *Today's Education,* January, 1972.
Codden, Vivian. "Yes To Love And Joyful Faces." *Life Magazine,* December 17, 1971.
Day, Beth. "With Love From ——." *Woman's Day,* December, 1970.
Di Leo, Joseph. *Children And Their Drawings,* Brummer/Mazel Publishers, 1970.
English and Foster. *Fathers Are Parents Too,* Belmont Books, 1962.
Epstein, Edward. "Where The Fine Arts Can Flourish." *Today's Education,* October, 1970.
"Family Relationships In The School." *Today's Education,* December, 1970.
Fremon, Suzanne. "New Ways To Measure Intelligence In Infants." *Parents Magazine,* April, 1971.
Geiser, Robert. "The Other Curriculum." *Grade Teacher,* November, 1971.
Ginott, Haim. *Between Parent And Child,* Avon Publishers.
Greenblatt, Augusta. "Hidden Handicap To Learning." *Parents Magazine,* October, 1970.
Gregg, Elizabeth. *What To Do When There's Nothing To Do,* Dell Publishing Inc., 1968.
Greiner, Charles. "Are You Listening To Or Talking At?" *Today's Education,* November, 1971.
Holt, John. *How Children Learn,* Pitman Publishing, 1967.
Howes, Virgil. *Individualization Of Instruction,* Macmillan Company, 1970.
Klein, David. "Exploding The Myth Of I.Q." *Parents Magazine,* October, 1971.

Krech, David. "Don't Use The Kitchen Sink Approach." *Today's Education,* October, 1970.

Lange, Cynthia. "The Crucial Years Of Learning." *Parents Magazine,* September, 1970.

Larrick, Nancy. *A Parent's Guide To Children's Reading,* Simon and Schuster, 1964.

Lewis and Reinach. *Looking And Listening,* McGraw Hill, 1966.

Mlynarczyk, Rebecca. "How Well Does Your Baby See?" *Parents Magazine,* October, 1971.

"Myself" and "Myself And Others." *Human Value Series,* Steck Vaughn Publishers, 1970.

O'Donnell, Taylor and McElaney. *Help Your Child Succeed In School,* Dell Publishing, 1962.

"Patterning." *Family Weekly,* September 13, 1970.

Pines, Maya. "A Child's Mind Is Shaped Before Age 2." *Life Magazine,* December 17, 1971.

Pines, Maya. "Teach Your Child To Behave Morally." *Readers' Digest,* October, 1970.

Postman. "The New Literacy." *Grade Teacher,* March, 1971.

Ratz, Margaret. "Keys To Success In Learning." *Parents Magazine,* October, 1971.

Sieber, Joan. "The Anxious Child." *Today's Education,* October, 1970.

Spock, Benjamin. "Play, How Much And What Kind?" *Redbook,* December, 1970.

Steinberg, Stephen. "The Language Of Prejudice." *Today's Education,* February, 1971.

Swyers, Betty. "Must They Conform?" *Grade Teacher,* February, 1971.

"Tips For Moms And Dads." *Ladies' Home Journal,* Hawthorne Books, 1970.

Wagar, J. Alan. "The Challenge Of Environmental Education." *Today's Education,* December, 1970.

Wyden, Barbara. "45 Crucial Months." *Life Magazine,* December, 1971.